100 Fresh and Fun
Handmade Cards

Step-by-Step Instructions for **50** New Designs and **50** Amazing Alternatives

by Kimber McGray

NORTH LIGHT BOOKS

CINCINNATI, OHIO
www.createmixedmedia.com

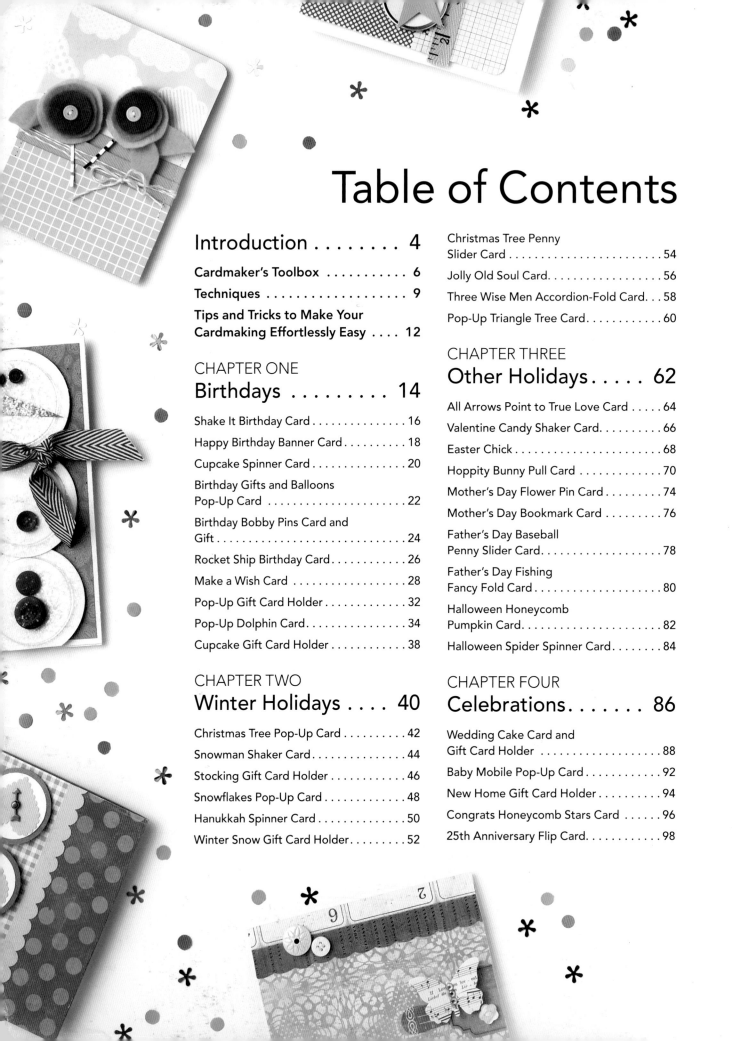

Table of Contents

CHAPTER FIVE
All Occasions 112

Introduction

As we continue to live in a world in which birthdays are celebrated with a quick message on Facebook and gift cards are the go-to presents for every occasion, there is no better way to stand out from the crowd and show your friends and family how much you care than by creating and sending handmade cards.

After writing *175 Fresh Card Ideas*, I felt I wanted to take cardmaking a step further and create innovative ways to include gifts, gift cards and interactive components in a variety of fun, customizable cards suitable for almost any occasion. In this book you will learn how to make a great basic card and then you'll learn how to turn it into an interactive card with parts that flip, fold, spin, shake, push, pull and pop up. Most of these cards use the same basic supplies, and wonderful stepped-out photos will help the beginner cardmaker create cards that look complex but are really quite simple.

And I know time is tight. Sometimes all you need is a quick card for a friend to let her know you are thinking about her; you'll find that here. But sometimes you want to create a more interactive card to entertain and bring a smile to a loved one's face. You'll find that here, too.

So bring out your inner child, play with some paper and see where your creative imagination takes you. You'll impress even yourself with the great cards you can make in minutes.

Card Maker's Toolbox

Compared to the amount of materials necessary for some crafts, the supplies you need to make beautiful cards are relatively few. But within this basic list, including paper, punches and embellishments, your options are almost unlimited. Add your fabulous imagination, and you'll be making beautiful handmade cards in no time!

Papers

Paper can bring a lot to a design, whether it be whimsy, beauty or even structure. There are two types of paper you'll need to made cards.

Heavyweight cardstock is the base of your card design. The heavier weight cardstocks will hold up better to mailing and general handling than thinner weight paper like designer paper or patterned paper. Cardstock between 60 lb. and 80 lb. (13gsm and 168gsm) will fold nicely and provide a strong base for your designs. Anything heavier will be difficult to fold cleanly.

Patterned papers can give your card its personality. There are so many different designs and styles that it can be a bit overwhelming at times. Just go with what you like and what fits the style of the cards you create. You can't go wrong.

Stamps and Inks

Stamps add a variety of figures, flourishes and words to your cards. The inks you choose will depend on the colors and look you want.

Rubber stamps are the most durable type of stamps and tend to produce the cleanest and sharpest images. Rubber stamps can come either premounted on a woodblock or unmounted, with or without a layer of foam. The foam is an important component of a clean-stamped image. If you purchase unmounted rubber stamps, you can buy foam to layer between the rubber stamp piece and the mounting block.

Clear stamps have benefits and challenges. It's much easier to see where you are placing your stamp image since you can see through the stamp. But clear stamps aren't as durable as rubber stamps, and they need to be stored properly for the longest usage life. Store them on a smooth, nonporous surface to keep them clean. If they don't stick to the mounting block, you can wash them with mild soap and warm water and let them air-dry.

All stamps should be stored out of direct heat and direct sunlight, as these elements can deteriorate the stamps.

When it comes to inks for the stamps, you can find many types of inks and a wide variety of colors.

Here are some of the most basic categories.

Dye ink dries quickly and can absorb into the paper, depending on the brand. These inks come in a variety of colors. Read the labels carefully to find out if the ink you choose is waterproof or not.

Pigment ink provides a more vibrant image. Because the ink sits on the surface of the paper, it dries more slowly, making it ideal for heat embossing. Heat setting will help the ink dry more quickly.

Chalk ink gives a softer, more blurred image. It is best used for coloring the edges of paper because it gives a soft, blended effect.

Embellishments

The key to embellishing cards is to keep the items you add light; heavy embellishments can bend the paper and create unwanted creases. The following embellishments can add a ton of visual—sometimes even dimensional—punch without weighing the card down.

Ribbons and trims offer endless choices. While you can find many varieties in paper stores, check out your local fabric stores as well. Silk and grosgrain ribbons create beautiful bows, while twills and twines are great for masculine cards.

Buttons are a nice flat embellishment to add to your card for a finishing touch. You can find buttons almost everywhere; paper stores and fabric stores carry nice selections. You can even salvage buttons from old clothing.

Chipboard pieces come in all shapes and sizes. They offer quick solutions for cardmakers who want to add dimension to their cards, and they are easy to decorate and match to card designs. You can also find predecorated chipboard shapes; look around and see if they inspire a card design.

Embossed embellishments can add delicious texture to card designs. Dry embossing leaves an imprint on the paper, and it can be created a few different ways. A simple way is to use brass stencils and a stylus. Another option is to use one of the many new machines and tools on the market; these machines make it almost foolproof and offer a wide variety of designs.

Heat embossing creates a smooth, raised image. You need a few items to add heat embossing to a card. You'll need a stamp of your choosing, a pigment ink or an embossing ink, and embossing powder. A heat gun is used to melt the embossing powder into a smooth, raised image.

Pens and markers can help add details and colors. Copic markers are increasingly being found in cardmakers' toolboxes because they produce beautiful colors and shading, and they have a high archival qulity.

A **basic sewing machine** can do double duty securing elements to and decorating your cards with straight and zigzag stitches. If you don't have a basic sewing machine, you can hand stitch with a **needle and thread**, or draw faux stitches on your cards with a pen or marker as a substitution.

Adhesives

Adhesives take your pretty designs and hold them together. You'll want a variety of adhesives on hand to tackle any design situation.

Dry adhesives, such as permanent tape runners, are for adhering decorative papers to the front of cards. **Wet adhesives,** including liquid glue and glue sticks, are also for adhering decorative papers to the front of cards, but you should use them sparingly because too much wet glue can cause the papers to curl.

Foam adhesive, often called "pop-up tape," allows you to add dimension to your designs. Foam adhesives come in a range of thicknesses to give your embellishments height.

Adhesive dots (like Glue Dots) are perfect for adhering small embellishments, such as buttons, to the card front.

Basic Tools

Basic punches and dies are some of the most used items in a cardmaker's toolbox. I recommend a corner rounder punch as well as a few sizes of circle and square punches. **Border punches** create a shaped border, like scallops, that add a nice touch to card designs.

Scissors are a mainstay for any cardmaker. You will probably want a variety of scissors that can add details. I recommend having one pair of detail scissors for cutting into small areas of paper and another pair of scissors dedicated to cutting ribbons and trims. Ribbon scissors should be used for only ribbons because paper would dull their blades, making it difficult to cut ribbon properly.

A **basic paper trimmer** that can cut a 12" × 12" (30.5cm × 30.5cm) or an 8½" × 11" (21.6cm × 28cm) piece of paper is a necessity. If you don't purchase premade card blanks, you will need to cut the paper down to the right size. Paper trimmers make these cuts more quickly and equally than hand cutting.

A **craft knife** is nice to have in your toolbox to use for cutting when scissors prove to be too bulky. Keeping a few extra blades on hand is a good idea, because fresh blades make cutting easier.

A **scoring tool** can create a crease in the paper for a clean and crisp fold. Many paper trimmers come with scoring blades you can use in conjunction with your trimmers. You can also use a **bone folder** and a **ruler** to score papers. Before folding a piece of paper in half to create a card blank, use a scoring tool to create the crease, allowing for a clean fold line. This can help keep some cardstocks from cracking when folded. There are a few different methods to create the crease, but I'll show you my favorite method on page 9 using a Scor-Pal.

Techniques

As with every craft, there are a handful of basic techniques you'll need to know that you'll see pop up over and over again. Once you've mastered the techniques on the next few pages, you'll be ready to tackle something, well, a little more interactive.

Making a Card Base

Creating a standard A2 sized, 5½" × 4¼" (14cm × 10.8cm), card blank from a piece of cardstock is as simple as one, two, three. And it's a good thing, too, since you'll find yourself returning to this technique for almost every card you make!

WHAT YOU'LL NEED

- ✪ Cardstock
- ✪ Paper trimmer
- ✪ Scoring tool (Scor-Pal is a good one)
- ✪ Bone folder

1 If you have a piece of 8½" × 11" (21.6cm × 28cm) cardstock, cut it in half to 5½" × 8½" (14cm × 21.6cm). If you have a 12" × 12" (30.5cm × 30.5cm) piece of cardstock, cut it down to 8½" × 11" (21.5cm × 28cm), and then cut it in half to 5½" × 8½" (14cm × 21.6cm).

2 Place the 5½" × 8½" (14cm × 21.6cm) piece of cardstock onto the scoring tool and square the edges of the paper to the sides of the scoring tool. Using the pointed end of the bone folder, score the length of the cardstock at the 4¼" (10.8cm) mark.

3 Remove the cardstock from the scoring tool and fold the cardstock at the score. Using the side of the bone folder, crease the cardstock at the fold.

Penny Sliders

Penny sliders are a great way to add a fun twist to your cards, and it is easier to make penny sliders than you might expect. In this book we feature three interchangeable techniques—choose the one that's right for you.

   The most important thing to watch out for when creating the channel for your penny sliders is to make sure it is wide enough to allow the piece of foam adhesive between the pennies to slide effortlessly without it being so large that your penny can slide right out of the channel.

Paper Punch Slider

It's easy to make penny sliders using specially designed paper punches. In the *Christmas Tree Penny Slider Card* (page 54), Lily Jackson uses one punch to make three different sized sliders, and the process is almost effortless.

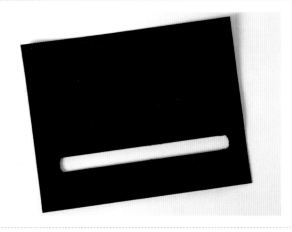

Die-Cutting Machine Software

With this technique, you will have perfect slots ever time. In the *Halloween Spider Spinner Card* (page 84), designer Nichol Magouirk uses software for a Silhouette cutter to make customized slots—this slot was programmed for a specific length and width.

Hand Drawn

Here's a penny slider technique that requires no special tools or appliances—just a steady hand. It is used to great effect in the *Father's Day Baseball Penny Slider Card* (page 78), and like the other techniques, this one is a piece of cake! If you aren't completely comfortable with the idea of hand drawing your slider channel on your card front, you can create a template first and then trace that onto the card.

Pop-Ups

Knowing how to create pop-ups is definitely something you'll want to have in your toolbox, and like so many of the fun treats in this book, once you start, I bet you won't be able to stop.

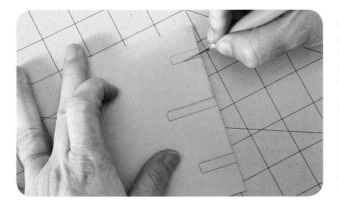

1 Mark two lines of equal length, parallel to each other, beginning in the fold of the card. Cut along the two parallel lines.

2 Score along the space between the cut lines. Fold along the scored lines, pushing the cut piece, or tab, to the interior of the card.

3 Cover the exterior of the card with paper to hide the cuts and serve as a base.

A GREAT EXAMPLE of this process is the *Snowflakes Pop-Up Card* on page 48. The pop-up mechanisms here are behind-the-scenes supports for items that will then be adhered to them.

The *Baby Mobile Pop-Up Card* on page 92 is also created in this same manner. Here, however, the pop-up mechanism is reinforced for strength and becomes a visible part of the card.

Another card in which the mechanisms become decorative elements is the *Birthday Gifts and Balloons Pop-Up Card* on page 22. Here the "gift" is cut flush to one edge of the card and the proportion is much larger than in the other cards. It is then decorated and additional pieces of folded cardstock are adhered to it to create the final scene.

And there's no rule that says the pop-up mechanisms need to be only square or rectangular in shape. The *Christmas Tree Pop-Up Card* on page 42 is a fun variation you make using the same steps of draw, cut, score and fold.

Tips and Tricks to Make Your Cardmaking Effortlessly Easy

There are many little tips for using your tools and supplies that you may not have thought about that will make your cardmaking a snap. Here are some of my favorite little tips and tricks that I rely on every day in my creating.

Circle Cutting

A circle cutter is a great way to create different sized circles for your projects without buying a lot of different sized punches. To cut a circle out of a large piece of paper, you simply place your fingers on the ring and press firmly as you rotate the blade around in a circular motion. The pressure from your fingers on the ring keeps your paper from moving while you cut.

Many times, though, you don't have a full sheet of paper to cut a circle out of. So how do you keep your paper from sliding around as you try to rotate the blade? Try putting a little bit of repositionable adhesive on the back of your piece of paper and pressing it onto your cutting mat. This will help keep your paper in place as you cut out your circle.

Paper Punching

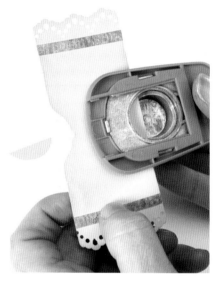

The biggest trick to using punches of any kind is to turn the punch upside down so you are looking at the bottom when you go to punch your paper. Doing this will allow you to see where and what you are going to punch, such as a specific image or word from a piece of paper or even just a bit of the paper to make a notch. I know it sounds so simple but it makes such a big difference in making sure you get what you want from your punch.

Working with Adhesive Dots

Adhesive dots let you make a strong instant bond to both slick surfaces and paper without the mess or the wait time of traditional adhesive. They are especially great for small items such as gems, small punched pieces and buttons. Here's a quick and easy way to add embroidery floss to a button. (Use this tip when it's time to embellish the Valentine's Day card on page 66.)

1 Run floss through the button and then lay the back of the button on an adhesive dot.

2 Tuck the ends of the floss into the adhesive dot and then adhere the button directly to your project.

Placing Small Pieces

Sometimes manipulating small embellishments can be difficult. Use the tip of your scissors or craft knife to aid you in the placement of these tiny items. Simply touch the tip of your blade to the adhesive on the back of the item, position the item into place, gently press it down with your fingertip and then pull your blade away.

Craft Knife Tips

Your craft knife should be one of the most vital tools in your toolbox, and with these great tips you'll be using it every time you craft.

1. Make sure you change your blade frequently. A craft knife shouldn't take a lot of effort to cut paper. If you find you have to press hard to make a cut, it's time to change the blade. A sharp blade makes a huge difference.

2. When cutting with a craft knife, cut into a self-healing mat or onto a glass cutting mat for best results. Not only will these things protect your work surface, they will also help you make better, cleaner cuts because they are meant to be used with a craft knife.

3. When cutting a curve with a craft knife, move your paper, not your knife. As you start along the curve, drag your knife to make the cut but once you have reached a point where your hand is moving almost upside down, slide the paper, keeping the hand holding the knife still and steady. You'll end up with a smoother line.

Birthdays

BIRTHDAYS ARE FUN DAYS full of cake, ice cream and cards! When birthdays roll around, we all love going to the mailbox to see if there's a card for us, bringing with it best wishes from afar.

In this chapter you will find cards that span the ages and delight both the young and the young at heart. Discover beautiful basic cards and cards that will really WOW! We've created cards that double as fun games and cards that incorporate either a small gift or a gift card. Others practically shout a hearty happy birthday with a festive banner or celebratory balloons. Something as simple as using elastic thread can make a sweet treat spin and twirl. We'll even show you how to make a cool card that might just grant a wish when the birthday boy or girl blows out a paper flame. We've got dolphins wearing birthday hats while they jump in the air and rockets that blast off with a single pull of a tab. And finally, we share a few ways to incorporate gift cards, such as hiding them in big oversized cupcakes covered in gemstone sprinkles.

Imagine the delight when someone you love receives such an amazing card created by YOU.

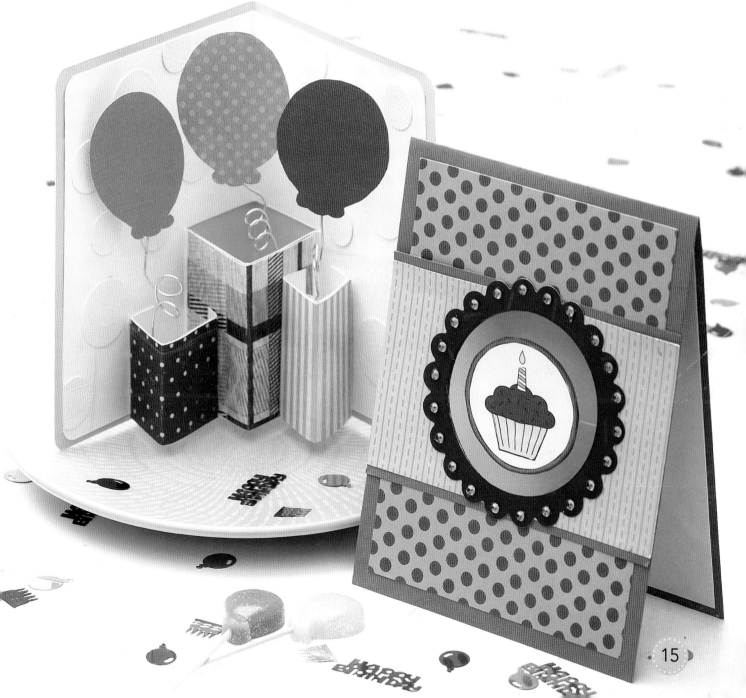

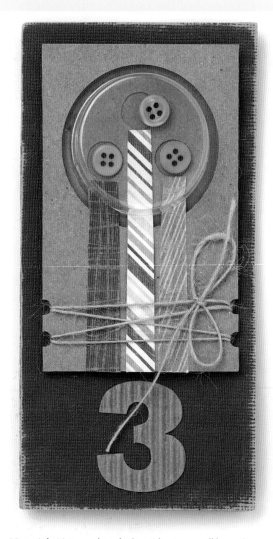

Shake It Birthday Card

By Sarah Hodgkinson

Let this cute card light up their big day! It becomes even more fun when you transform the basic card into a shaker game. (And feel free to customize the card to whichever age is appropriate for your recipient.)

WHAT YOU'LL NEED

- Cardstock
- Sandpaper
- Paper trimmer
- Paper punch
- Patterned paper
- Adhesive
- Buttons
- Twine
- Die-cut number
- Circle punch
- Craft knife
- Pencil
- Shaker cup

Materials List *cardstock*: Core'dinations, Jillibean Soup; *patterned paper*: Jillibean Soup, Fancy Pants Designs; *die cuts*: Jillibean Soup; *twine*: Jillibean Soup; *floss*: DMC; *buttons*: Buttons Galore; *clear cup*: Stampin' Up!; *punches*: EK Success, We R Memory Keepers, Fiskars; *other tools*: Core'dinations Sand It Gadget, Xyron craft knife

The Basics

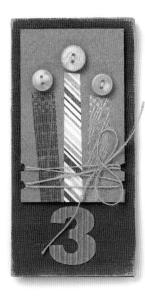

1. Create the 3" × 6" (7.6cm × 15.2cm) card base by folding a 6" × 6" (15.2cm ×15.2cm) square of brown cardstock in half. Lightly sand the edges to distress them.
2. Cut a 2½" × 4" (6.4cm × 10.2cm) piece of Kraft cardstock.
3. Using a hole punch, punch half circles to create notches on each side, ¼" (6mm) and ½" (12mm) up from the bottom.
4. Cut three strips of patterned paper to approximately ½" × 3" (12mm × 7.6cm). You'll want a little variation in size here. Adhere the strips to the Kraft cardstock.
5. Adhere the buttons to the top of the patterned paper strips to create candles.
6. Wrap 15" (38cm) of twine around the bottom of the Kraft cardstock and through the notches you created in Step 3. Tie the twine into a bow on the front of the cardstock. Adhere the cardstock to the card base.
7. Adhere the die-cut number to the card base, below the cardstock.

Beyond the Basics

To Start:

Follow steps 1–3 of **The Basics.** Cut an additional two pieces of cardstock (you'll be working with a total of three), each measuring 2" × 2" (5cm × 5cm). Cut the three strips of patterned paper but do not adhere them.

1 Punch a 1¾" (4.5cm) circle in one of the pieces of Kraft cardstock, about ¼" (6mm) from the top. This will be Layer A of the cardstock.

2 Cut a slit in the cup with a craft knife. The slit should be large enough to accommodate the paper candles.

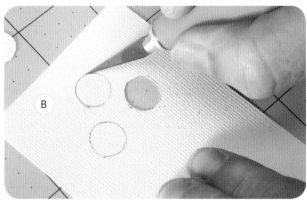

3 Lay the buttons on one of the smaller pieces of Kraft cardstock and trace around them with a pencil. This will be Layer B of the cardstock.

4 Cut out the holes for the buttons with a craft knife.

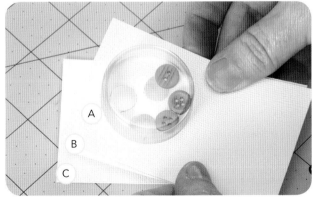

5 Assemble the shaker by placing the buttons in the cup. Place the cup through the punched circle in Layer A, positioning the slit at six o'clock. Adhere Layer B behind Layer A. Then, adhere the remaining piece of Kraft cardstock (Layer C) behind Layer B.

To Finish:

Adhere the bottom half of the patterned paper candles to Layer A of the Kraft cardstock. Carefully insert the top parts of the candles into the cup through the slit. Follow steps 6–7 to finish the card.

Happy Birthday Banner Card

By Kimber McGray

Birthdays are banner days. Celebrate by stringing up a breezy banner card full of color and whimsy.

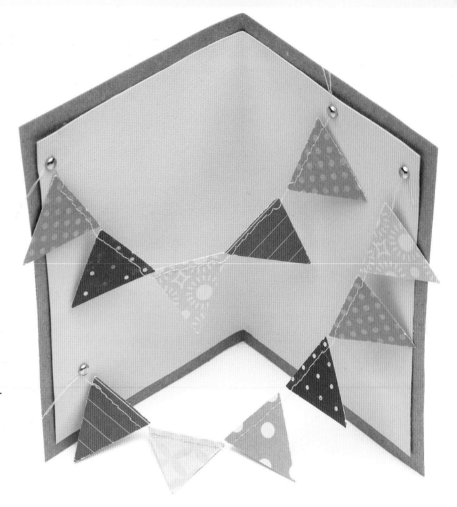

WHAT YOU'LL NEED

- Cardstock
- Gel pen
- Triangle punch
- Patterned paper
- Thread and sewing machine
- Adhesive
- Buttons
- Stickers
- Paper Trimmer
- Paper piercer
- Decorative brads

Materials List *Cardstock:* Jillibean Soup, Core'dinations; *patterned paper:* Crate Paper, BoBunny Press; *punch:* Fiskars; brads: Making Memories; *sticker:* Jenni Bowlin Studios; button: American Crafts; *pen:* Uniball Signo; *sewing machine:* Singer; *thread:* Coats & Clark

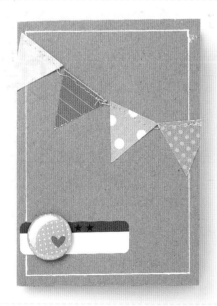

The Basics

1. Start with a standard A2 Kraft card base (4¼" × 5½" [10.8cm × 14cm]).
2. Draw a border ¼" (6mm) around the card base with a white gel pen.
3. Punch triangles from patterned paper. Machine stitch the triangles together to make a banner. Adhere the banner to the card.
4. Embellish the card with buttons and stickers.

Beyond
the Basics

To Start:
Follow steps 1–4 from **The Basics** to make the card front.

1 Punch triangles from patterned paper—eleven or twelve should do the trick.

2 Machine stitch the triangles together to create two banners. Leave a length of extra thread on the ends of the banners. Do not trim.

3 Cut an 8" × 5" (20.3cm × 12.7cm) piece of patterned paper to use as a card liner. Pierce holes in the card liner to accommodate the brads.

4 Insert the brads and flatten the backs of the brads behind the liner.

5 Adhere the liner to the interior of the card base.

6 Wrap the ends of the sewn banner threads around the brads to secure.

Cupcake Spinner Card

By Rae Barthel

What a sweet treat to receive a card that has as many wonderful details as this one!

WHAT YOU'LL NEED

- Cardstock
- Paper trimmer
- Patterned paper
- Adhesive
- Scissors
- Circle cutter
- Ink
- Border punch
- Rhinestones
- Elastic cord
- Tape

The Basics

1. Make a 6" × 4½" (15.2cm × 11.4cm) card base from pink cardstock. (This card will open vertically.)
2. Cut a 4" × 5½" (10.2cm × 14cm) piece of polka-dot patterned paper and adhere it to the center of the card.
3. Cut a piece of stripe-patterned paper to 4½" × 2¾" (11.4cm × 7cm) and mat with a piece of pink cardstock cut to 4½" × 3" (11.4cm × 7.6cm). Adhere this panel to the card.
4. Cut a circle (approximately 1¾" [4.5cm]) from patterned paper, centering any dominant design in the center of the circle, and ink the edges of the circle.
5. Cut a circle (about ¼" [6mm] larger than your patterned paper circle) from pink cardstock, and cut a scalloped circle (about ⅜" [1.0cm] larger than the previous circle) from brown cardstock.
6. Adhere all three circles together and then adhere this piece to the card.
7. Adhere rhinestones to the scalloped circle.

   (See the basic card on page 21.)

Materials List *cardstock:* Hobby Lobby; *patterned paper:* Nikki Sivils Scrapbooker; *rhinestones:* Michaels Stores; *dies:* Spellbinders; *die-cutting tool:* Cuttlebug by Provo Craft; *stretch cord:* Pepperell; *ink:* Clearsnap

Beyond the Basics

To Start:

Follow steps 1–5 from **The Basics.** For this version of the card, you will need two circles of the size cut in step 4.

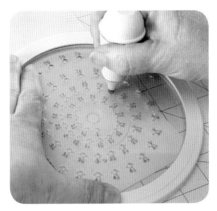

1 Cut a circle out of center of the front of the card base. The circle should be about ¾" (2cm) larger than the circle you cut from patterned paper.

2 Tape an elastic cord (about 4" [10.2m]) to the back of one of the circles from step 4 in **The Basics**.

3 Adhere elastics to the interior of the card with tape.

4 Cover the taped elastic with cardstock pieces. Adhere the second circle to the first to cover the taped elastic.

To Finish:

Adhere the scalloped circle to the card base, around the edges of the circle cutout, and adhere rhinestones to the scalloped circle. Line the interior of the card with a contrasting color of cardstock or patterned paper.

Tip

If your patterned paper circles have a dominant image (like the cupcakes in the main project card), be sure to adhere them together so that the image lines up correctly when spun on the elastic. You wouldn't want one of your cupcakes to look like it's upside down when it's spinning, for example.

Birthday Gifts and Balloons Pop-Up Card

By Kimber McGray

Nothing says birthday more than balloons. This card is sure to delight when the balloons appear to float out of wrapped birthday gifts.

Materials List *cardstock:* Core'dinations; *patterned paper:* BasicGrey, BoBunny Press, Crate Paper; *punches:* EK Success, Stampin' Up!; *wire:* Michaels Stores

WHAT YOU'LL NEED

- ✪ Cardstock
- ✪ Paper trimmer
- ✪ Corner rounder
- ✪ Patterned paper
- ✪ Adhesive
- ✪ Border punch
- ✪ Craft knife
- ✪ Black pen
- ✪ Wire
- ✪ Pencil
- ✪ Tape
- ✪ Foam adhesive
- ✪ Bone folder

The Basics

1. Create a standard A2 card base from yellow cardstock (4" × 5½" [10.2cm × 14cm]) and round the right-side corners.

2. Cut a piece of patterned paper to 4½" × 3½" (11.4cm × 9cm) and round the right-side corners. Adhere a 4½" × ½" (11.4cm × 1.3cm) strip of scalloped white cardstock to the back of the patterned paper and adhere the patterned paper piece to the front of the card.

3. Using the template on page 138, cut out a balloon from green patterned paper. Outline the balloon with a black pen.

4. Create a metal tail for the balloon by wrapping wire (approximately 6" [15.2cm]) long) around a pencil. Press the wire to flatten, and attach it to the back of the balloon with a piece of tape. Adhere the balloon to the front of the card with foam adhesive.

Beyond the Basics

To Start:
Make the front of the card according to the instructions for **The Basics.** Then...

1 Cut a 8" × 5" (20.3cm × 12.7cm) card liner from white cardstock. Mark a line on the back of the card liner 2½" (6.4cm) from bottom and 1½" (3.8cm) to the right of the fold. Cut on the 1½" (3.8cm) long line.

2 Score on the 2½" (6.4cm) line.

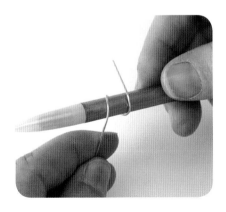

3 Fold along the score line to create a pop-up box inside the folded liner.

4 Cut a piece of patterned paper to 2½" × 3" (6.4cm × 7.6cm) and adhere it to the pop-up box on the interior of the card. Create two more boxes by cutting a 2" × 3" (5cm × 7.6cm) piece of white cardstock and score at ½", 1½" and 2½" (1.3cm, 3.8cm and 6.4cm), and a 1½" × 3" (4.8cm × 7.6cm) piece of white cardstock and score at ½", 1½" and 2½" (1.25cm, 4cm and 6cm).

5 Create curly wires for the balloons by wrapping craft wire around a pencil. Pull the wire off the pencil and press it flat.

6 Cut out balloon shapes, adhere the shapes to wire and secure the wire to the back of the boxes with tape.

7 Cover the smaller boxes with patterned paper and adhere the tabs to the liner and the center box. Adhere the liner to the body of the card.

Birthday Bobby Pins Card and Gift

By Summer Fullerton

These adorable posies are sweet enough as an embellishment, but bobby pins? Any little girl (and some big girls, too!) will fall in love with these.

Materials List *Card base:* Jillibean Soup; patterned *paper:* Jillibean Soup; *ribbon:* Jillibean Soup; *twine:* Jillibean Soup; *felt:* Jo-Ann Fabric and Craft Stores; *buttons:* Fancy Pants Designs; *floss:* DMC; *bobby pins:* Horizon Fabric

WHAT YOU'LL NEED

- Cardstock
- Paper trimmer
- Patterned paper
- Scissors
- Ribbon
- Adhesive
- Twine
- Circle cutter
- Felt
- Buttons
- Thread and sewing machine
- Hot glue
- Bobby pins
- Corner rounder punch

The Basics

1. Create a 4" × 5½" (10.2cm × 14cm) card base from cardstock.
2. Cut a piece of cloud patterned paper to 4" × 4" (10.2cm × 10.2cm) and adhere it to the top of the card.
3. Cut two 4" (10.2cm) pieces of green ribbon. Adhere one strip of ribbon 2¾" (7cm) from the bottom of the card.
4. Cut a piece of green grid-patterned paper to 4" × 3" (10.2cm × 7.6cm), and adhere the second strip of ribbon across the top edge of this piece. Wrap baker's twine three times around the ribbon and tie into a bow on the front of the ribbon.
5. Adhere the green grid-patterned paper to the bottom of the card.
6. To make the flowers, cut two sets of three different-sized circles from three different shades of blue felt, and layer the felt circles together. Cut three leaves from green felt. Stitch a small button in the center of the circles and stitch the leaves to the back of the flowers. (See step 2 of *Beyond the Basics*.)
7. Adhere felt flowers to the card front with glue.

Beyond the Basics

To Start:

Follow steps 1–3 from **The Basics.** Attach the first piece of ribbon only to the left and right edges of the card. Then follow step 4.

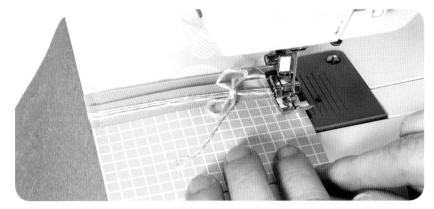

1 Adhere the green grid-patterned paper to the card base, adhering only the sides and bottom edges to create a pocket. Machine stitch all the layers along the sides to secure the pocket.

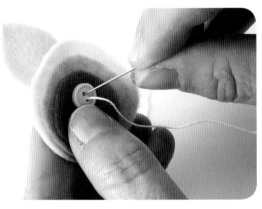

2 To create the felt flower bobby pins, cut different-sized circles and leaves from felt and stitch together with a button.

3 Adhere the felt flower to a bobby pin with hot glue.

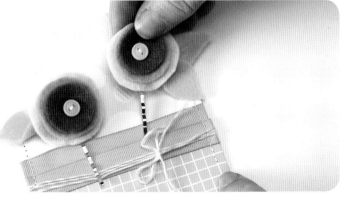

4 Slide the finished felt bobby pins in the front pocket of the card.

To Finish:

Round the corners of the card with a corner rounder punch.

Rocket Ship Birthday Card

By Kimber McGray

5, 4, 3, 2, 1. . . Blast off to birthday fun with a card that is out of this world!

WHAT YOU'LL NEED

- ✪ Cardstock
- ✪ Paper trimmer
- ✪ Stamp
- ✪ Ink pads
- ✪ Markers
- ✪ Craft knife
- ✪ Foam adhesive
- ✪ Black pen
- ✪ Chipboard
- ✪ Adhesive
- ✪ Bone folder
- ✪ Pencil

The Basics

1. Create a 4" × 5" (10.2cm × 12.7cm) card base from light blue cardstock.

2. Stamp a rocket ship image on white cardstock, color the image with markers and then cut it out. Stamp, color and cut out a few extra flames. Adhere the images to the card with foam adhesive.

3. Draw scrolls with a black pen.

4. Color chipboard scrolls with a white ink pad. Adhere the chipboard pieces to the card.

(See the basic card on page 14.)

Materials List *cardstock:* Core'dinations; *stamp:* Bella Blvd by Unity Stamp Company; *ink:* Momento by Tsukineko, Maya Road; *markers:* Copic; *chipboard:* Maya Road; *foam adhesive squares:* 3L Scrapbook Adhesives

Beyond the Basics

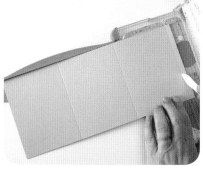

1 Cut a piece of cardstock to 5" × 11½" (12.7cm × 29.2cm). From the left, score at 3¾", 7½" and 11¼" (9.5cm, 19cm and 28.6cm).

2 Rotate the card base 90 degrees and score at ¼" (6mm) along both long sides.

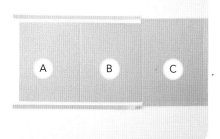

3 Fold along the three shorter score lines and trim off the cardstock along the ¼" (6mm) score lines on panels A and B.

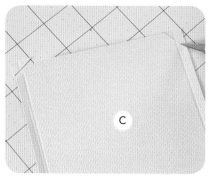

4 Notch the corners of Panel C.

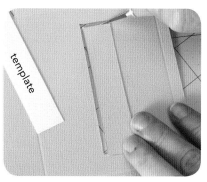

5 Cut a template from cardstock to ¾" × 3½" (2cm × 9cm). Place the template on Panel C, 1½" (3.8cm) from the bottom. Trace around the template and then cut it out.

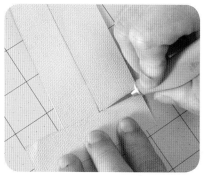

6 Create a slide pull from a piece of cardstock cut to 4¾" × 3" (12cm × 7.6cm). From this piece, cut a "T." The legs of the "T" should each measure 1" (2.5cm).

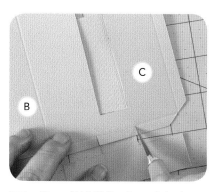

7 Cut a 1¼" (3.2cm) notch in the ¼" (6mm) scored area at the bottom of Panel C. The slide pull will slide through this notch when the card is done.

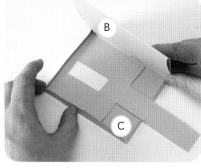

8 Fold the ¼" (6mm) tabs to the interior of the card, as shown, and adhere Panel C to Panel B, with the slide pull installed as shown.

9 Create the rocket ship embellishment as per step 2 of **The Basics**. Adhere the chipboard scrolls to the back of the embellishment, and adhere the embellishment to the slide with foam adhesive. Adhere the extra flames to the cardstock behind the slide.

Make a Wish Card

By Kelly Goree

Make a wish and blow out the candles! With a simple tug, the flame on this fancy card disappears. Wouldn't both the young and the young at heart love this card?

WHAT YOU'LL NEED

- Cardstock
- Paper trimmer
- Patterned paper
- Adhesive
- Brown marker
- Corner rounder punch
- Border punch
- Foam adhesive
- Pencil
- Craft knife
- Glitter glue
- Circle punch
- Gel pen (optional)

Materials List *cardstock:* Bazzill Basics; *patterned paper:* My Mind's Eye; *pen:* Zig, Uni-Ball Signo; *stickles:* Ranger; *punches:* Fiskars, Creative Memories

The Basics

1. Create a 5" × 7" (12.7cm × 17.8cm) card base from red cardstock.

2. Adhere a 4½" × 6½" (11.4cm × 16.5cm) piece of floral patterned paper to the center of the card front. Draw faux-stitching around the edges of the patterned paper with a brown marker.

3. Cut a 3½" × 5" (9cm × 12.7cm) piece of green patterned paper and round the top corners (see template on page 137).

4. Scallop the edge of a 7" × 1" (17.8cm × 2.5cm) piece of pink patterned paper and cut it in half. Layer and adhere the strips on the bottom of the green patterned-paper panel.

5. Adhere a 3½" × ½" (9cm × 1.3cm) strip of stripe-patterned paper over the scalloped strips. Faux-stitch a line along the top edge with a brown marker.

6. Adhere the green patterned paper panel to the front of the card with foam adhesive.

7. Using the template on page 137, cut the bottom of the cupcake out of brown patterned paper. Add dashed lines with a white gel pen if desired. Adhere to the card front.

8. Cut a ½" × 2" (1.3cm × 5cm) strip of stripe-patterned paper and adhere it to the card for the candle.

9. Using the template, cut out the top of the cupcake from pink patterned paper. Adhere it to the card.

10. Using the template, cut out the swirl from pink polka-dot patterned paper and adhere it to the card front with foam adhesive. Add a little bit of glitter glue on each of the polka dots.

11. Cut out two flames from yellow patterned paper, one slightly larger than the other. Adhere the larger flame to the card directly above the candle, and then adhere the smaller flame on top of the larger flame with foam adhesive.

Beyond the Basics

To Start:
Follow steps 1–5 from **The Basics.**

1 With a craft knife, cut two horizontal slits just larger than 1" (2.5cm) in the middle of the green patterned paper (see template on page 137), about 1½" (3.8cm) from the top and 1" (2.5cm) from the bottom. Here, I'm doing the cutting on the back side of the patterned paper.

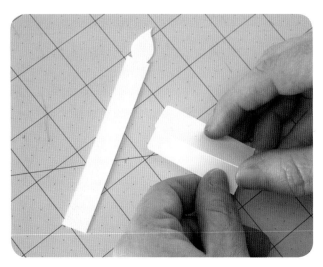

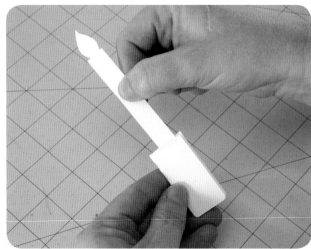

2 Create a candle out of white cardstock and cover the flame with patterned paper (use the template on page 137). Cut a piece of white cardstock to 2" × 2" (5cm × 5cm). Fold the cardstock in half so that it measures 1" × 2" (2.5cm × 5cm). This will be your pull tab.

3 Adhere the pull tab to the bottom of the candle, extending it ½" (1.3cm) below the bottom of the candle, and round the bottom corners of the tab. The total length of the candle with the pull tab attached should be 4¾" (12cm).

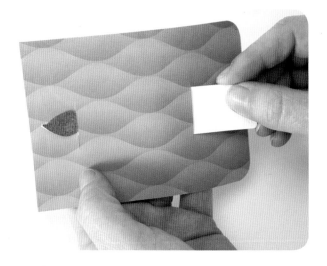

4 Create the cupcake using the template on page 137. Cut the flame off the long candle and cover the rest of this candle with patterned paper to create the "flameless" candle. Adhere this to the back of the cupcake, not to the back of the "flamed" candle.

5 Slide the candle through the slits on the 3½" × 5" (9cm × 12.7cm) piece of patterned paper, as shown. Adhere this piece to the card.

To Finish:

Finish embellishing the card by using the template to cut out just the swirl of the cupcake and the cupcake liner from coordinating patterned paper. Adhere both to the card with foam adhesive.

6 Adhere over the interactive candle portion, lining up the non-flame candle with the flamed candle. Notch the bottom of the cupcake using a 1" (2.5cm) circle punch. Adhere the notched cupcake over the interactive candle portion, lining up the flames.

Pop-Up Gift Card Holder

By Kimber McGray

They'll flip when they find a gift card inside this great card! With a little tug on the ends, a gift card will pop out and surprise your friend.

WHAT YOU'LL NEED

- ✪ Cardstock
- ✪ Paper trimmer
- ✪ Patterned paper
- ✪ Adhesive
- ✪ Border punch
- ✪ Circle cutter
- ✪ Ink pads
- ✪ Corrugated die-cut shape
- ✪ Button
- ✪ Foam adhesive
- ✪ Craft knife
- ✪ Corner punch
- ✪ Bone folder

The Basics

1. Create a standard A2 card base (4¼" × 5½" [10.8cm × 14cm]) from white cardstock.
2. Cut five strips of coordinating patterned paper to 1" × 4¼" (2.5cm × 10.8cm). Adhere the strips to the card base.
3. Adhere a yellow scalloped strip of cardstock, 4" × ½" (10.2cm × 1.3cm), under a 4" × ½" (10.2cm × 1.3cm) piece of patterned paper, staggering the two slightly, and adhere to the card.
4. Cut a 1¾" (4.5cm) diameter ring from brown cardstock and adhere it to the front of the card.
5. Ink the top of a corrugated cardboard star with a white ink pad. Add a small button and adhere the star to the front of the card with a foam adhesive square.
6. Finally, punch the corners of the card with a ticket notch punch.

(See the basic card on page 33.)

Materials List
cardstock: Bazzill Basics, Core'dinations; *patterned paper:* Jillibean Soup; *punches:* Stampin' Up!; *corrugated shape:* Jillibean Soup; *ink:* Maya Road; *button:* Nikki Sivils Scrapbooker

Beyond the Basics

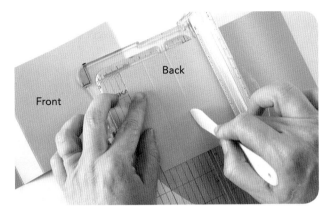

1 Cut two pieces of cardstock to 4¼" × 7" (10.8cm × 17.8cm). Score at 1" (2.5cm) and 2" (5cm) on each piece, from the left side of the cardstock.

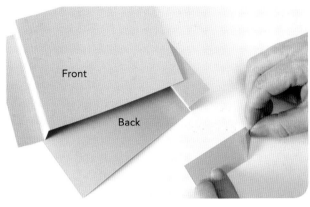

2 Create the pop-up piece—cut a strip of cardstock to 1" × 3" (2.5cm × 7.6cm) and fold a 1" (2.5cm) triangle into one end, creating a flap.

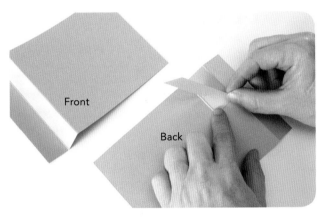

3 Adhere the flap to the second fold on the back piece of cardstock, ½" (1.3cm) down from the top.

4 Adhere the cardstock pieces together as shown.

5 Use removable adhesive to adhere a gift card to the pop-up piece.

To Finish:
Embellish the front (and sides) of the card following the directions for **The Basics.** The pop-up card in this project uses eight strips of patterned paper (seven on the front and one on the right side behind the brown strip).

Pop-Up Dolphin Card

By Nichol Magouirk

Who doesn't love a sweet dolphin? Add a googly eye and a festive party hat and he will be the hit of the party! You can also create an interactive version of the card. Your card will dazzle when that same sweet dolphin appears to leap out of the water and off the card!

WHAT YOU'LL NEED

- Cardstock
- Paper trimmer
- Stamps
- Ink pad
- Adhesive
- Thread and sewing machine
- Baker's twine
- Dies and die-cut machine
- Markers
- Craft knife
- Googly eyes
- Pom-pom
- Circle punch
- Pencil
- Bone folder
- Hole punch

Materials List *card base:* Hero Arts; *cardstock:* Neenah; *stamps:* Lawn Fawn, Papertrey Ink, Hero Arts; *ink:* Memento by Tsukineko, Stampin' Up!; *markers:* Copic; *glossy medium:* Ranger Glossy Accents; *gemstones:* Hero Arts; *eye:* Hobby Lobby; *twine:* Divine Twine; *ribbon:* Stampin' Up!; *dies:* Papertrey Ink; *punches:* EK Success

The Basics

1. Trim ¼" (6mm) off the top of a standard A2 card base (4¼" × 5½" [10.8cm × 14cm]) and stamp with a polka dot stamp.
2. Cut a piece of white cardstock 3" × 3¾" (7.6cm × 9.5cm) and a piece of black cardstock 2¾" × 3¼" (7cm × 8.3cm). Adhere the black cardstock to the white cardstock.
3. Machine stitch around the edges of the cardstock panel, wrap the panel with baker's twine and adhere it to the front of the card.
4. Die cut a label shape from light blue cardstock and stamp it with a coordinating stamp.
5. Die cut a scalloped circle from a darker blue cardstock and adhere it to the center of the label.
6. Die cut a circle from white cardstock and stamp with it with blue waves. Adhere this circle to the center of the scalloped circle.
7. Adhere the layered label panel to the cardstock panel.
8. Stamp a dolphin and a party hat onto white cardstock and color the images with markers. Cut out and adhere the pieces to the card, on top of the circle. Add a googly eye and pom-pom to embellish.
9. Add glossy accents to some of the background-stamped images so they look like bubbles.

Beyond the Basics

1 Trim ¼" (6mm) off the top of a standard A2 card base (4¼" × 5½" [10.8cm × 14cm]).

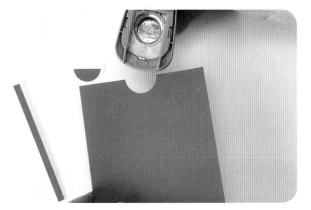

2 Notch the top center of the card with a 1" (2.5cm) circle punch.

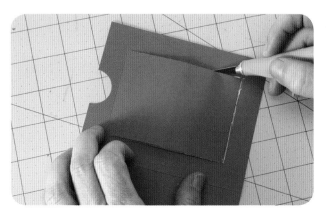

3 Draw a line ½" (1.3cm) in from the edge on all four sides of the front of the card. Score along the top marked line. With a craft knife, cut along the other three marked sides, leaving the scored line intact.

4 Score a line in the center of the cut panel.

5 Adhere the front and back of the card together, along the side and bottom edges, creating a pocket at the top of the card.

6 Create the tag by cutting a piece of light blue cardstock to 3" × 5¼" (7.6cm × 13.3cm). Next, create a ½" (1.3cm) circle tab and punch a hole in it with a standard sized hole punch. Adhere the circle tab to the top of the cardstock.

7 Clip the bottom two corners. Score the tag ½" (1.3cm) from the bottom edge.

8 Slide the tag into the card base through the pocket. Fold the tag along the score line, and adhere the ½" (1cm) tab to the back of the bottom edge of the cut panel of the card base.

To Finish:
Follow steps 3–9 of **The Basics** to embellish the card. Embellish the inside of the pocket with more fish, and tie a piece of twine through the hole in the circle tab.

9 Cut a piece of black cardstock to 2¾" × 3½" (7cm × 9cm) and mat it with a piece of cream cardstock cut to 3" × 3¾" (7.6cm × 9.5cm). Machine stitch around the edges of the matted pieces, if desired. Adhere this piece to the bottom half of the cut panel on the front of the card, lining up the bottom edges.

Cupcake Gift Card Holder

By Lisa Dorsey

A sweet treat with a surprise all its own? Yes, please!

WHAT YOU'LL NEED

- Cardstock
- Paper trimmer
- Patterned paper
- Adhesive

- Decorative edged scissors
- Pencil
- Craft Knife
- Embossing folder
- Chalk ink

- Gemstones
- Adhesive dots
- Sewing machine and thread (optional)

Materials List *cardstock:* Bazzill Basics; *patterned paper:* The Paper Studio; *embossing folder:* Sizzix; *gemstones:* Creative Charms; *ink:* Clearsnap; *adhesive dots:* Glue Dots International

The Basics

1. Create a 5½" × 6" (14cm × 15.2cm) card base from red cardstock.
2. Cut a piece of polka-dot patterned paper to 5⅛" × 5¾" (13cm × 14.6cm) and adhere it to the front of the card.
3. Using decorative edged scissors, cut a piece of green cardstock to 5⅛" × 4½" (13cm × 11.4cm). Add machine stitching, if desired. Adhere the cardstock to the card.
4. Using the template on page 137, cut the bottom of the cupcake from red patterned paper and adhere it to the card.
5. Using the template on page 137, cut the top of the cupcake from yellow cardstock and dry emboss it. Ink the edges of the cupcake top and adhere it to the card.
6. Cut a cherry shape and adhere it to the top of the cupcake.
7. Embellish the cupcake with gemstones.

Beyond the Basics

To Start:
Follow steps 1–7 from **The Basics,** but do not adhere the cupcake top or bottom to the card base. Instead...

1 Create a pocket with the cupcake base by adhering only the sides and bottom to the card base.

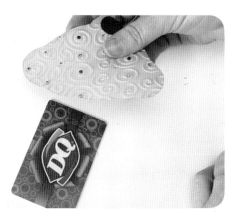

2 Attach a gift card to the back of the cupcake top using adhesive dots. Leave the bottom of the gift card exposed.

3 Slide the gift card into the pocket to hold the cupcake top in place.

2

Winter Holidays

TIS THE SEASON for keeping in touch with family and friends. In this chapter you will find great resources for creating simple cards—the kind you can mass produce when your holiday card list numbers in the dozens or more. There's a sweet snowman made from simple punched circles and buttons, and there's a beautiful nativity scene accordion card created quickly and easily with stamped images. Of course you will also find in this chapter lots of great cards that shake, pop and roll. Check out the Christmas tree card with penny slider ornaments, the beautiful, rustic pop-up snowflake card, the Santa pop-up card and the spinning Hanukkah card. And we've also included a few different options for giving gift cards, including a traditional stocking created from paper. Now, who wouldn't like to find that hung by the chimney with care?

Christmas Tree Pop-Up Card

By Kimber McGray

Nothing says Christmas more than the classic colors of rich red and evergreen mixed with traditional plaid and poinsettias. Imagine the surprise when your loved one opens this card and a Christmas tree appears, adorned with beautiful bulbs and topped with a gold star.

Materials List *cardstock:* Core'dinations; *patterned paper:* BasicGrey, BoBunny Press; *punches:* EK Success, Stampin' Up!, Marvy Uchida; *twine:* BasicGrey; *pearls:* BasicGrey; *pen:* Uni-Ball Signo; *foam adhesive squares:* 3L Scrapbook Adhesives

WHAT YOU'LL NEED

- Cardstock
- Paper trimmer
- Corner rounder
- Patterned paper
- Adhesive
- Border punch
- White gel pen
- Scissors
- Foam adhesive
- Pencil
- Bone folder
- Twine
- Self-adhesive pearls
- Craft knife

The Basics

1. Create a standard A2 card base (4¼" × 5½" [10.8cm × 14cm]) from red cardstock. Round the upper and lower right corners with a corner rounder.
2. Cut a 3" × 4¼" (7.6cm × 10.8cm) piece of plaid patterned paper and adhere it to the bottom of the card. Round the lower right corner with a corner rounder.
3. Cut a 4¼" × ½" (10.8cm × 1.3cm) scalloped border from green patterned paper using a scalloped border punch. Adhere the border to the card, along the top edge of the plaid paper.
4. With a white gel pen, faux stitch a line above the green patterned paper border.
5. Cut out two poinsettia flowers from patterned paper. Leave one whole and cut out the inner flower from the design on the second one. Adhere the two flowers together with foam adhesive. Adhere the flowers to the card.

Beyond the Basics

To Start:

Make the front of the card following the instructions for **The Basics.**

1 For the card liner, cut patterned paper to 5" × 7½" (12.7cm × 19cm) and round the corners. With a pencil, mark 1¼" (3.2cm) from the bottom and 2" (5cm) out from each side of the center fold. Draw a straight line connecting the two marks to create a triangle.

2 Make a mark ½" (1.3cm) from the bottom with a pencil. Draw an arc going through the mark connecting the bottom corners of the triangle.

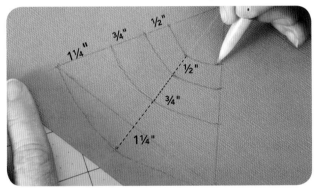

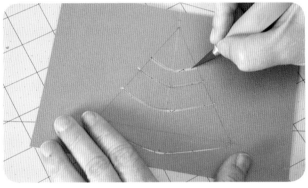

3 Mark the other tiers of the tree: 1¼" (3.2cm) up from the bottom on each side and up from the bottom of the curve on the fold. Join all three marks to create the next arc; ¾" (2cm) up from the last marks on the sides, connect with an arc; ½" (1.3cm) up from the last marks on the sides connect with an arc.

4 Cut each arc from left to right along the arc lines with a craft knife.

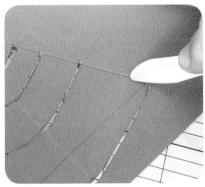

5 Score from the top of the tree down to the lower corners of the tree.

6 Push the tree to the inside of the card to create the pop up. Then adhere the liner to the interior of the card base.

To Finish:

Embellish the interior of the card as shown in the photo on page 42.

Snowman Shaker Card

By Kimber McGray

This sweet snowman card will warm your heart. Simple punched circles and basic buttons come together to create a homespun friend. Adhering simple shaker containers over the circles and adding a dash of sparkling glitter brings him to life right before your eyes.

WHAT YOU'LL NEED

- Cardstock
- Paper trimmer
- Patterned paper
- Adhesive
- Border punch
- Baker's twine
- Circle punch
- Buttons
- Ribbon
- Shaker pouches
- Glitter
- Foam adhesive

Materials List *cardstock:* Core'dinations; *patterned paper:* Jillibean Soup; *twine:* Jillibean Soup; *buttons:* Stampin' Up!; *ribbon:* May Arts; *plastic cup:* Stampin' Up!; *punches:* EK Success, Stampin' Up!; *foam adhesive squares:* 3L Scrapbook Adhesives; *glitter:* Our Craft Lounge

The Basics

1. Create a standard A2 card base (4¼" × 5½" [10.8cm × 14cm]) from white cardstock.

2. Cut a piece of patterned Kraft paper to 4¼" × 5½" (10.8cm × 14cm) and adhere it to the card.

3. Scallop the edge of a 5¼" × 1½" (13.3cm × 3.8cm) piece of red cardstock. Adhere it to the front of the card, along the left edge. Wrap baker's twine around the card three times and tie a bow on the front of the card.

4. Cut three 2½" (6.4cm) circles from white cardstock and adhere them to the front of the card with foam adhesive, overlapping the circles slightly. Trim a bit off the bottom circle if it hangs off the edge of the card.

5. Adhere buttons and a red ribbon scarf to the circles to create a snowman.

6. Cut a small triangle from orange cardstock and adhere it for the nose.

Beyond the Basics

To Start:
Create a card base to measure 3½" × 7" (9cm ×17.8cm). Cut a piece of patterned Kraft paper to 3¼" × 6¾" (8.3cm × 17cm) and adhere it to the card base. Scallop the edge of a ½" × 6¾" (1.3cm × 17cm) piece of red cardstock and adhere it along the left edge of the card base. Wrap baker's twine around the card three times and tie a bow on the front of the card. Then...

1 Cut three circles from white cardstock to match the size of the shaker pouches. Glue buttons and a nose onto the various circles. Then fill the shaker pouches with glitter.

To Finish:
Adhere the pouches to the card base with foam adhesive, and adhere a ribbon scarf to the snowman.

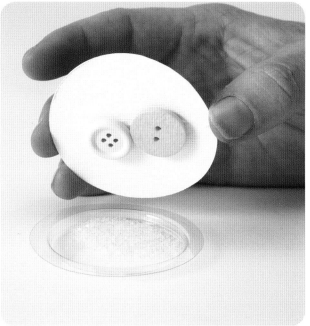

2 Remove the backing from the shaker pouch adhesive and adhere the cardstock circles to the pouches. (Adhere cardstock to the pouches to avoid spilling the glitter—once it's free, it can't ever be fully contained again!).

Stocking Gift Card Holder

By Kimber McGray

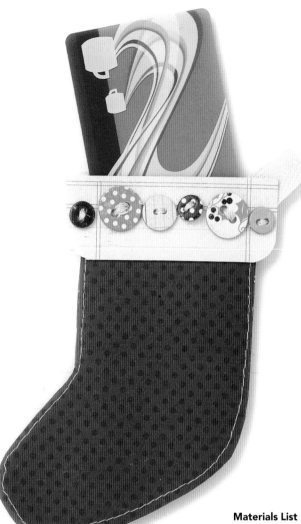

Some stockings are hung by the chimney with care. This one is filled with a gift card. This is a unique way to present a gift card using a traditional icon of Christmas.

WHAT YOU'LL NEED

- ✪ A2 card base
- ✪ Patterned paper
- ✪ Paper trimmer
- ✪ Pencil
- ✪ Scissors
- ✪ White gel pen
- ✪ Corner rounder
- ✪ Adhesive
- ✪ Twill tape
- ✪ Chipboard buttons
- ✪ Sewing machine and thread (optional)

Materials List *cardstock:* Jillibean Soup; *patterned paper:* Making Memories, BoBunny Press, My Mind's Eye; *buttons:* Making Memories; *pen:* Uni-Ball Signo; *sewing machine:* Singer; *thread:* Coats & Clark; *twill:* Creative Impressions; *floss:* DMC

The Basics

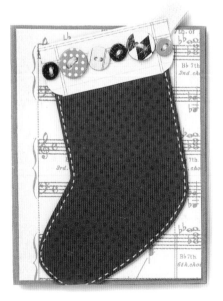

1. Begin with a standard A2 Kraft card base (4¼" × 5½" [10.8m × 14cm]).
2. Adhere a 4" × 5¼" (10.2cm × 13.3cm) piece of patterned paper to the card base.
3. Using the template on page 136, cut out a stocking from red patterned paper. Faux stitch around the edges of the stocking with a white gel pen.
4. Cut a strip of patterned paper to 1½" × 3" (3.8cm × 7.6cm), round the bottom corners of the strip and adhere it to the top edge of the stocking.
5. Fold a small piece of twill tape to form a loop, and adhere the loop to the back of the stocking.
6. Adhere the stocking to the front of the card and embellish the top edge with chipboard buttons.

Beyond the Basics

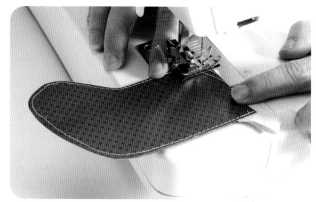

1 Using the template on page 136, cut out two stockings from patterned paper. Remember to flip the template over before cutting out the second stocking so the stockings are mirror images. This will allow the "right sides" of the patterned paper to be on the outside of the finished stocking.

2 Adhere the wrong sides of the stockings together around the outside edges only, leaving the top edge open. Or, if desired, machine stitch the stockings together with an ⅛" (3mm) seam allowance, again, along all edges except the top.

3 Embellish the front of the stocking as instructed in steps 3–6 of **The Basics.** Finally, slide a gift card into the stocking.

Snowflakes Pop-Up Card

By Lily Jackson

These felt snowflakes might melt your heart, but they'll never melt in your hand.

Materials List *cardstock:* Gina K. Designs; *patterned paper:* Cosmo Cricket, BasicGrey; *pearls:* Recollections; *ribbon:* Craft Supply

The Basics

1. Create a standard A2 card base (4¼" × 5½" [10.8cm × 14cm]) from white cardstock. Distress the edges.
2. Cut a piece of pink patterned paper to 3¾" × 5" (9.5cm × 12.7cm) piece of pink patterned paper. Distress the edges.
3. Cut a piece of sheer ribbon 4½" (11.4cm) long. Tie a knot in the ribbon, slightly off center. Wrap the ribbon around the pink patterned paper and adhere the ends to the back of the patterned paper. Adhere the patterned paper to the card.
4. Embellish the card with a few swirls cut from green patterned paper. Glue a pearl to the center of a felt snowflake and adhere it over the knot in the ribbon.

WHAT YOU'LL NEED

- Cardstock
- Paper trimmer
- Sandpaper
- Patterned paper
- Ribbon
- Scissors
- Adhesive
- Self-adhesive pearl
- Felt snowflakes
- Pencil
- Craft knife
- Circle punch

Beyond the Basics

To Start:

Make the front of the card following the instructions for **The Basics.** Then...

1 Cut a cardstock liner to 4¾" × 8" (12cm × 20.3cm). Fold the liner in half. With a pencil, mark three different sets of pop-up hinges on the back of the folded liner, each ¼" (6mm) wide and varying in length from ¾" to 1¾" (2cm to 4.5cm). Cut along the length of the hinges but be sure not to cut along the ¼" (6mm) measures.

2 Open the liner and push the hinges in to the interior of the card liner.

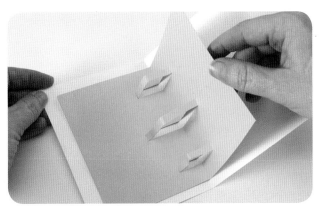

3 Adhere the liner to the inside of the card base.

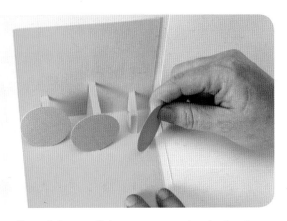

4 Adhere felt snowflakes to appropriately sized patterned paper circles, and then adhere the snowflakes to the hinges. Adhere a 4¾" × ½" (12cm × 1.3cm) scalloped patterned paper strip to the bottom edge of the card liner.

Hanukkah Spinner Card

By Kimber McGray

Light up the night of a cherished friend or family member with this unique "spin" on the tradition of lighting the menorah.

WHAT YOU'LL NEED

- Card base
- Cardstock
- Paper trimmer
- Circle punches
- Adhesive
- White gel pen
- Pencil
- Craft knife
- Paper piercer
- Brad

Materials List *cardstock:* Core'dinations; *brad:* Making Memories; *punches:* EK Success, Marvy Uchida

The Basics

1. Start with a standard A2 navy blue card base (4¼" × 5½" [10.8m × 14cm]).

2. Make a menorah: Cut a ¼" × 3" (6mm × 7.6cm) strip of silver cardstock for the base of the menorah. From silver cardstock, punch a 1½" [3.8cm] circle and cut a segment from that circle that is equal to about one-third for the menorah stand.

3. Cut eight ¼" × 1¼" (6mm × 3.2cm) pieces of white cardstock and one ¼" × 1½" (6mm × 3.8cm) piece of white cardstock for the candles.

4. Adhere all pieces to the card base, as shown. Draw candlewicks with a white gel pen.

5. Cut nine candle flames from yellow cardstock and adhere to the top of the candlewicks.

Beyond the Basics

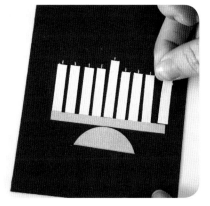

1 Follow steps 1–4 of **The Basics.**

2 Using a 3½" (9cm) circle as a template, draw an arc with a pencil centered above the candles.

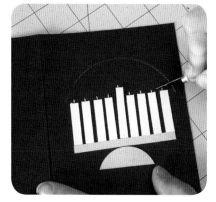

3 Cut along the arc line and along a straight line above the center candlewick to create a window.

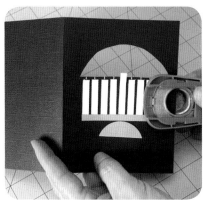

4 Create a notch on the right side of the card front using a 1" (2.5cm) circle punch.

5 Place a blue 4" (10.2cm) circle behind the window and pierce a hole through the center of the middle candle and through the 4" (10.2cm) circle.

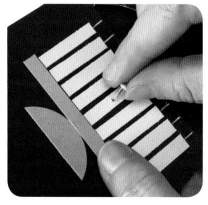

6 Insert a white brad into the hole and through the front of the card and the 4" (10.2cm) circle.

7 Adhere one candle flame to the blue circle directly above the middle candle.

8 Rotate the 4" (10.2cm) circle 180 degrees and add nine flames, one above each candle, for a fully lit menorah.

Winter Snow Gift Card Holder

By Kimber McGray

While the winter winds blow outside, send a beautiful blue and white card covered in pearl swirls to keep in touch with a special friend over the winter holidays.

Materials List *cardstock:* Core'dinations; *patterned paper:* BoBunny Press; *ribbon:* Bazzill Basics; *punches:* Stampin' Up!, EK Success; *gemstones:* Zva Creative

WHAT YOU'LL NEED

- ✪ Cardstock
- ✪ Paper trimmer
- ✪ Patterned paper
- ✪ Adhesive
- ✪ Border punch
- ✪ Self-adhesive pearl swirls
- ✪ Ribbon
- ✪ Scissors
- ✪ Corner rounder
- ✪ Bone folder
- ✪ Craft knife

The Basics

1. Begin with a standard A2 white card base (5½" × 4¼" [14cm × 10.8cm]).

2. Cut a piece of stripe-patterned paper to 4¼" × 5½" (10.8cm × 14cm), and adhere it to the card.

3. Cut a 5½" × 1" (14cm × 2.5cm) strip of white patterned paper. Using a border punch, scallop one edge. Adhere the strip to the front of the card.

4. Embellish the card with a self-adhesive pearl swirl.

5. Tie a ribbon around the card and in a bow.

6. Round the bottom corners of the card with a corner rounder.

Beyond
the Basics

To Start:
Follow all **The Basics** steps to
make the card front. Then...

1 Cut two 1" × 3¼" (2.5cm × 8.3cm) strips of white
cardstock. Score each from the left edge at 1", 1¼",
2¼" and 2½" (2.5cm, 3.2cm, 5.7cm and 6.4cm).

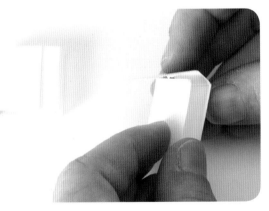

2 Fold and adhere the ¾" (2cm) side to the 1"
(2.5cm) side to create blocks.

3 Adhere the blocks to the interior of the card base.

4 Cut a 5" × 5½" (12.7cm × 14cm) piece of patterned paper and scallop the top edge. Score 1"
(2.5cm) from the top edge. Adhere the paper to
the interior of the card, lining up the bottom edge
of the paper with the bottom edge of the card.
The score line should fit neatly against the blocks
and the remaining inch (2.5cm) will fit to the top
of the blocks, creating the gift card holder. Cut a
piece of patterned paper to 3¼" × 5½" (8.3cm
× 14cm) and adhere it to the top of the interior
of the card. Round the corners and embellish the
interior with ribbon and self-adhesive pearls.

Christmas Tree Penny Slider Card

By Lily Jackson

Adorning a Christmas tree is a fun holiday tradition. Creating a card with penny slider ornaments is almost as much fun. Tilt the card from side to side to see the Christmas balls move across the tree.

WHAT YOU'LL NEED

- ✪ Cardstock
- ✪ Paper trimmer
- ✪ Sandpaper
- ✪ Patterned paper
- ✪ Adhesive
- ✪ Pencil
- ✪ Craft knife
- ✪ Circle punch
- ✪ Foam adhesive
- ✪ Slot punch
- ✪ Pennies

Materials List *cardstock:* Gina K. Designs, DCWV; *patterned paper:* Cosmo Cricket; *paper distresser:* Tim Holtz; *punch:* Stampin'Up!

The Basics

1. Create a standard A2 card base (4¼" × 5½" [10.8cm × 14cm]). Distress the edges, if desired.
2. Cut a piece of green patterned paper to 3¾" × 5" (9.5cm × 12.7cm) and distress the edges. Adhere it to the card front.
3. Cut a triangle from a piece of yellow patterned paper. The triangle should measure 3½" (9cm) at its widest point and 4½" (11.4cm) at its tallest point. Adhere the triangle to the card.
4. Punch three small circles from coordinating patterned paper, distress the edges and adhere the circles to the front of the card with foam adhesive.

Beyond the Basics

To Start:
Follow steps 1–3 for **The Basics,** but do not adhere the triangle to the card. Instead...

1 Use a slider punch to create a horizontal opening in the center of the triangle. (In all, you will create three slider openings.)

2 For the bottom slider opening, you will need to punch multiple times—line up the punch carefully and take your time.

3 For the top row, use one of the waste punch pieces from a previous step. Fold it to create a shorter channel and use it as a template. Cut this channel with a craft knife.

4 Create three penny sliders by sandwiching foam adhesive between two pennies.

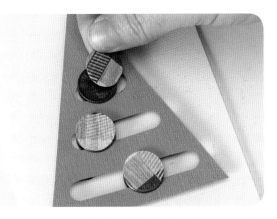

5 Adhere the tree to the card with two layers of foam adhesive, stacked one on top of the other. Carefully slip the penny sliders into the channels.

6 Cover the penny sliders with circles of patterned paper so they resemble ornaments.

Jolly Old Soul Card

By Kimber McGray

You just never know when Santa Claus will pop up and surprise you! This time around, he's here to spread some holiday cheer ... but only if you've been nice.

Materials List *cardstock:* Jillibean Soup, Core'dinations; *Santa embellishment:* Hobby Lobby; *punch:* Martha Stewart; *glitter:* Hobby Lobby; *gemstones:* Queen & Co; *foam adhesive squares:* 3L Scrapbook Adhesives

WHAT YOU'LL NEED

- A2 Kraft card base
- Cardstock
- Craft knife
- Adhesive
- Glitter glue pen
- Adhesive foam squares
- Santa embellishment
- Snowflake punch
- Bone folder
- Gemstones

56

The Basics

1. Start with a standard A2 Kraft card base (4¼" × 5½" [10.8cm × 14cm]).
2. Cut a piece of embossed red cardstock to 3¾" × 2¼" (9.5cm × 5.7cm). Hand cut a strip of white cardstock to 4½" (11.4cm). Hand scallop the edge of the strip so it resembles snow. Adhere the strip to the chimney. Embellish with a glitter glue pen.
3. Adhere the cardstock chimney to the base card with adhesive foam squares. Adhere only along the edges of the chimney, being sure to leave an opening in which to insert a Santa embellishment.
4. Cut off as much of the bottom part of the Santa embellishment as necessary to fit it snugly into the chimney.
5. Adhere two snowflakes punched from white cardstock to the card base.

Beyond the Basics

1 Begin with a standard A2 Kraft card base. Cut a piece of embossed red cardstock to 3¾" × 2¼" (9.5cm × 5.7cm). Hand cut white cardstock to approximately 4½" (11.4cm) and hand scallop the edge. Adhere the white cardstock "snow" to the top edge of the chimney.

2 Using foam adhesive, adhere the cardstock chimney to the card base. Adhere only the edges, leaving an opening in which to place the Santa embellishment.

3 Cut a 1" × 5½" (2.5cm × 14cm) strip of Kraft cardstock. Score and fold one end at ¾" and 2½" (2cm and 6.4cm). Adhere the ¾" (2cm) tab to the inside of the card, 1¾" (4.5cm) from the top edge. Adhere the Santa embellishment to the lower half of the Kraft strip. Slide Santa's feet into the chimney.

To Finish:

Embellish the front of the card by creating another chimney with snow. Adhere a few die-cut snowflakes to both the interior and the front of the card. Add a little sparkle to the snowy chimneys with a glitter glue pen. Adhere various gemstones to the card for added shine and dimension.

Three Wise Men Accordion-Fold Card

By Kimber McGray

Spread the joy of the Christmas story with a rustic accordion-fold card.

WHAT YOU'LL NEED

- Cardstock
- Paper trimmer
- Patterned paper
- Twine
- Kraft tags
- Stamps
- Ink pads
- Markers
- Craft knife
- Foam adhesive
- Bone folder

Materials List *cardstock:* Jillibean Soup, Core'dinations; *patterned paper:* Jenni Bowlin Studio; *tags:* Jillibean Soup; *stamps:* Inkadinkado; *ink:* Memento by Tsukineko; *markers:* Copic; *twine:* Jillibean Soup

The Basics

1. Start with a standard A2 card base (4¼" × 5½" [10.8cm × 14cm]).
2. Cut a piece of patterned paper to 3¾" × 5" (9.5cm × 12.7cm) and adhere it to the card.
3. Tie twine around two Kraft tags and adhere the tags to the front of the card.
4. Stamp images onto white cardstock and color the images with markers.
5. Cut out the images and adhere them to the tags with foam adhesive.

Beyond the Basics

1 Start with a Kraft card base measuring 5½" × 11½" (14cm × 29.2cm). Score the card, from the left, at: 4¼", 4¾", 5¼", 5¾", 6¼", 6¾" and 7¼" (10.8cm, 12cm, 13.3cm, 14.6cm, 16cm, 17cm and 18.4cm).

2 Fold along the score marks to create a card that measures 5½" × 4¼" (14cm × 10.8cm). You will work with the accordion fold at the bottom of the card. Adhere a 24" (61cm) piece of twine around the length of the card, leaving approximately 6" (15.2cm) extending beyond the top and bottom of the card and including 2" (5cm) of slack along the accordion fold spine. Adhere a 3¾" × 5" (9.5cm × 12.7cm) piece of patterned paper to the front of the card and a 3¾" × 5" (9.5cm × 12.7cm) piece of cardstock to the back of the card.

3 Adhere a 3¾" × 5" (9cm × 12.7cm) piece of patterned paper to the inside of the card and adhere stamped embellishments to the patterned paper and in the valleys of the accordion folds to create your scene.

To Finish:
Embellish the front of the card with stamped images, Kraft tags and twine, as instructed in **The Basics.** Tie the 6" (15.2cm) of twine from the top and bottom of the card to close the finished card.

Pop-Up Triangle Tree Card

By Kimber McGray

By simply duplicating the same shape multiple times, you can easily create a pop-up element for a card. With this card, it's easy to see how a handful of triangles easily turn into a simple Christmas tree design.

Materials List *cardstock:* Jillibean Soup, Core'dinations; *patterned paper:* Jillibean Soup, BoBunny Press; *punches:* Marvy Uchida, Fiskars, EK Success; *twine:* Jillibean Soup; *foam adhesive squares:* 3L Scrapbook Adhesives

The Basics

1. Start with a standard A2 Kraft card base (4¼" × 5½" [10.8cm × 14cm]).

2. Cut a piece of Kraft cardstock to 5½" × 3½" (14cm × 9cm). Punch both long sides of the cardstock with a decorative border punch. Adhere the cardstock to the card base.

3. Cut a 5½" × 3" (14cm × 7.6cm) piece of patterned Kraft paper and adhere it to the card base. Using a white gel pen, add faux-stitching along the edge of the patterned Kraft paper.

4. Cut a triangle from a piece of green patterned paper; the triangle should measure 4" (10.2cm) at its widest point and 4½" (11.4cm) at its tallest point. Wrap twine around the triangle four or five times to mimic garland, and tie it into a bow on the front of the card. Adhere a piece of brown patterned paper cut to ¾" × 1" (2cm × 2.5cm) to the bottom of the patterned paper tree.

5. Adhere the tree to the front of the card with foam adhesive.

6. Punch a star out of yellow cardstock and adhere it to the top of the tree with a foam adhesive.

- ✪ Cardstock
- ✪ Patterned Kraft paper
- ✪ Paper trimmer
- ✪ Border punch
- ✪ Adhesive
- ✪ Patterned paper
- ✪ White gel pen
- ✪ Twine
- ✪ Foam adhesive
- ✪ Star or asterisk punch
- ✪ Corner rounder
- ✪ Bone folder

Beyond the Basics

To Start:
Following all steps for **The Basics**, create the front of the card. Cut a piece of patterned paper to 8" × 5" (20.3cm × 12.7cm), round all corners and adhere it to the interior of the card as the card liner. Then...

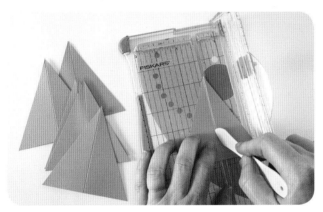

1 Cut six triangles from 4" × 4" (10.2cm × 10.2cm) pieces of green patterned paper. Score and fold each in half.

2 Adhere the wrong sides of the triangles together.

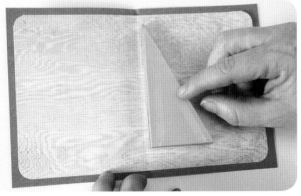

3 Adhere the two outermost pieces of the folded tree to the card liner, aligning the center of the tree with the center fold of the card.

To Finish:
Add a tree trunk and a star to the tree, and embellish it with paper-punched asterisk snowflakes decorated with a white gel pen.

Other Holidays

THROUGHOUT THE YEAR are so many great card-sending holidays, like Valentine's Day, Easter, Mother's Day, Father's Day and Halloween. And in this chapter we've got them all covered. How about giving a card filled with chocolate candies for Valentine's Day? Or sending a silly scary spider that slides across a card to surprise a little friend for Halloween? You can even send your mom a vintage-inspired bookmark tucked into a lace-embellished pocket for Mother's Day.

For another Mother's Day idea we'll show you how to create a beautiful felt flower pin that any mom would love. Suggest to Dad a trip to the ballpark to take in a game or a trip to the lake in hopes of hooking a big fish for Father's Day. Play with chalk cardstock and write an eerie Halloween message on a totally customizable card. And don't miss a certain sweet little peep that is about to come out of his shell just in time for Easter.

All Arrows Point to True Love Card

By Kimber McGray

Cupid didn't strike just once but three times. Watch Cupid's arrows spin round and round, pointing finally to your one true love. There is no doubt about how much you care when you send this love-filled card on Valentine's Day.

Materials List *cardstock:* Core'dinations, Jillibean Soup; *patterned paper:* Crate Paper; *punches:* Stampin' Up!, Fiskars, EK Success; *button:* Nikki Sivils Scrapbooker; *spinners:* Tim Holtz; *foam adhesive squares:* 3L Scrapbook Adhesives

The Basics

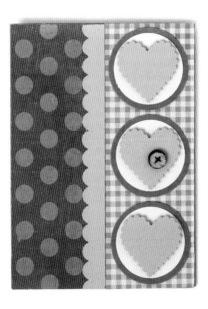

1. Begin with a standard A2 Kraft card base (4¼" × 5½" [10.8cm × 14cm]).
2. Cut and adhere a 2" × 5½" (5cm × 14cm) piece of pink polka-dot patterned paper to the left side of the card.
3. Cut and adhere a 2" × 5½" (5cm × 14cm) piece of pink gingham patterned paper to the right side of the card.
4. Cut a ½" × 5½" (1.3cm × 14cm) strip of pink cardstock and scallop one edge with a border punch. Adhere the strip over the area on the cardstock where the two patterned papers meet.
5. Punch three 1½" (3.8cm) circles from white cardstock and three 1¾" (4.5cm) circles from Kraft cardstock. Adhere the white circles to the Kraft circles and adhere the Kraft circles to the card.
6. Punch three hearts from pink cardstock and adhere them to the centers of the circles with foam adhesive.
7. Embellish the center heart with a button.

WHAT YOU'LL NEED

- ✪ Card base
- ✪ Paper trimmer
- ✪ Patterned paper
- ✪ Adhesive
- ✪ Cardstock
- ✪ Border punch
- ✪ Circle and heart punches
- ✪ Foam adhesive
- ✪ Buttons
- ✪ Thumbtack or paper piercer
- ✪ Arrow spinners
- ✪ Decorative brads

Beyond the Basics

To Start:

Follow **The Basics** through step 5, but don't adhere the circles to the card. Punch three hearts from pink cardstock and adhere them to the centers of the circles with regular adhesive, not foam adhesive. Then...

1 Pierce the centers of the circles with a thumbtack or paper piercer.

2 Attach spinners to the circles with brads.

3 Adhere the circles to the card with foam adhesive.

Valentine Candy Shaker Card

By Kimber McGray

This year, skip the big box of chocolates and the store-bought card. Create a great combination of both with a candy-filled heart set into a precious handmade card.

WHAT YOU'LL NEED

- Card base
- Paper trimmer
- Border punch
- Patterned paper
- Strong adhesive
- Cardstock
- Heart punch
- Buttons
- Thread
- Adhesive dots
- Foam adhesive
- Ribbon
- Scissors
- Candy holder
- Candy

Materials List *cardstock:* Core'dinations; *patterned paper:* BoBunny Press; *ribbon:* Creative Impressions; *plastic container:* BoBunny Press; *buttons:* Stampin' Up!, Buttons Galore; *foam adhesive squares:* 3L Scrapbook Adhesives

The Basics

1. Create a card base cut to 5" × 3¾" (12.7cm × 9.5cm). (This card will open vertically.)

2. Punch along the sides of the card base with a scalloped border punch.

3. Cut a piece of pink patterned paper to 3¾" × 5½" (9.5cm × 14cm), and adhere it to the card.

4. Cut a piece of white cardstock to 2¼" × 4¼" (5.7cm × 10.8cm) and adhere it to the pink patterned paper.

5. Punch two hearts from pink and white cardstock, the pink heart slightly larger than the white heart, and adhere the two together.

6. Adhere threaded buttons to the layered punched heart with glue dots and adhere the heart to the card with foam adhesive.

7. Tie a ribbon into a bow and adhere it to the front of the card with an adhesive dot.

Beyond the Basics

1 Create the same card base as for the basic card. Cut a piece of white cardstock to 2¼" × 4¼" (5.7cm × 10.8cm). Insert it into the back of a BoBunny candy holder.

2 Tie a ribbon through the hole in the front of the candy holder.

3 Fill the holder with candy and close it.

4 Adhere the candy holder to the front of the card with a strong adhesive.

Easter Chick Card

By Kim Hughes

Easter and spring are both known as times of birth and renewal. Tucked among the beautifully decorated eggs peeks out a chick about to hatch. With a gentle pull, the sweet peep is a great new friend to greet your loved one on Easter morning.

WHAT YOU'LL NEED

- ✪ Card base
- ✪ Paper trimmer
- ✪ Patterned paper
- ✪ Adhesive
- ✪ Border punch
- ✪ Foam adhesive
- ✪ Pencil
- ✪ Circle punch
- ✪ Scissors

Materials List *cardstock:* Core'dinations; *patterned paper:* Echo Park Paper, Cosmo Cricket, Doodlebug Design, My Mind's Eye, SEI; *punches:* Stampin' Up!, Marvy Uchida; *foam adhesive squares:* Zva Creative; *pen:* Sakura

The Basics

1. Create a card base cut to measure 4¼" × 4¾" (10.8cm × 12cm).

2. Cut a piece of green patterned paper to 4¼" × 5½" (10.8cm × 14cm) and adhere it to the card base.

3. Cut a piece of blue patterned paper to 4¼" × 2¾" (10.8cm × 7cm) and adhere to the top of the card base.

4. Cut a strip of green patterned paper to 4¼" × 1½" (10.8cm × 3.8cm), scallop one edge with a border punch and adhere it to the card with foam adhesive.

5. Using the whole-egg template on page 138, cut out three eggs from different patterned papers. Tuck the eggs behind the scalloped edge and adhere them to the card.

Beyond the Basics

To Start:
Follow all **The Basics** steps. Then...

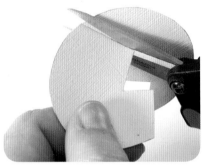

1 Trace and cut out one additional egg to match one you have already cut out. Cut a zigzag along the center of this egg to create a cracked egg. (Or, use the cracked-egg templates on page 138).

2 Make the chick out of a circle punched from yellow cardstock (1¾" [4.5cm]) and adhere wings made using the pattern on page 138. Cut a beak from patterned paper and draw eyes on the chick.

3 Adhere the top part of the cracked egg to the top of the chick.

4 Adhere the bottom of the cracked egg to the card with foam adhesive. Adhere only the sides and bottom of the cracked egg, leaving a pocket in which to insert the chick.

5 Slide the chick into the egg.

Hoppity Bunny Pull Card

By Kimber McGray

Here comes Peter Cottontail ... hopping right in to the hands of your favorite little one this Easter.

Materials List *cardstock:* Bazzill Basics; *patterned paper:* Pebbles Inc.; *punches:* Fiskars, Martha Stewart; *die cut:* K&Company

The Basics

1. Create a standard A2 card base from white cardstock (4¼" × 5½" [10.8cm × 14cm]).
2. Cut a piece of green patterned paper to 5" × 2½" (12.7cm × 6.4cm) and adhere it to the front of card.
3. Cut a strip of pink patterned paper to 5" × 1" (12.7cm × 2.5cm) and punch one edge with a decorative border punch. Adhere the strip to the card.
4. Cut a strip of floral patterned paper to ¼" × 5" (6mm × 12.7cm) and adhere it to the card.
5. Adhere the die-cut bunny to the front of the card with foam adhesive.
6. Punch a butterfly from orange patterned paper and adhere it to the front of the card with foam adhesive.
7. Hand draw dotted lines with a black pen to emulate the bunny's path.

Beyond the Basics

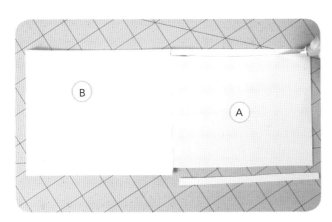

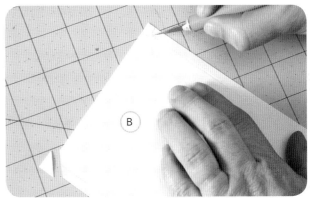

1 Create a standard A2 card base from white cardstock and set it aside (4¼" × 5½" [10.8cm × 14cm]). Then cut a piece of white cardstock to 4¾" × 11¼" (12cm × 28.6cm). Score at ¼" (6mm) along both long sides and one short side. Score at 5½" (14cm) from the unscored, short side. Trim off the ¼" (6mm) scored piece from the Panel A with a craft knife.

2 Trim the corners from Panel B with a craft knife.

3 Create a rectangle template measuring ¾" × 5" (2cm × 12.7cm). Place the template on Panel B, ½" (1.3cm) from the bottom edge and centered. Trace around the template with a pencil.

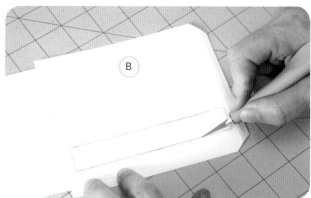

4 Using a craft knife, cut out the rectangle.

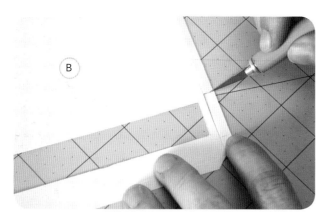

5 Using a craft knife, cut out a 1" (2.5cm) notch from the right edge of the cardstock, next to the rectangular opening (for the slide pull).

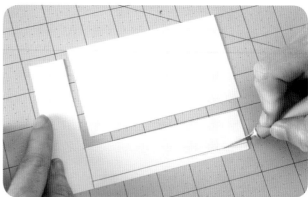

6 Create the slide from a 4" × 5¾" (10.2cm × 14.6cm) piece of white cardstock. The stop on the left is 1" (2.5cm) wide and the slide is 1" (2.5cm) wide. Cut off ¼" (6mm) from the bottom and 2¾" (7cm) from the top.

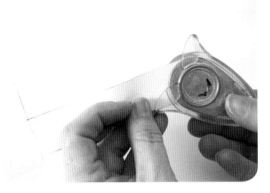

7 Round the corners of the slide with a corner rounder.

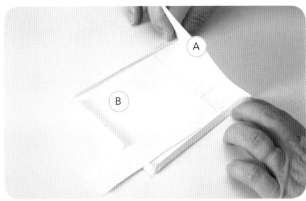

8 Fold up all scored pieces and add adhesive to the ¼" (6mm) tabs. Lay the slide in the notch. Adhere the panel edges together.

9 Adhere a die-cut bunny to the slide with foam adhesive.

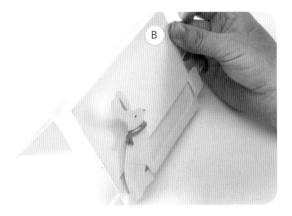

10 Adhere the slider portion of the card to the white card base.

To Finish:

Embellish the card with a piece of green patterned paper that measures 5" × 2½" (12.7cm × 6.4cm). Adhere it along the top edge of the slider panel. Punch a strip of pink patterned paper with a border punch and layer it behind a 5" × ½" (12.7cm × 1.3cm) strip of flower patterned paper. Adhere this piece along the bottom edge of the slider panel. Punch a butterfly from orange patterned paper and adhere it to the front of the card.

Finish the card by adding a dashed path with a black pen on the part of the card that shows when the slider pull is all the way open, as shown in the photo on page 70.

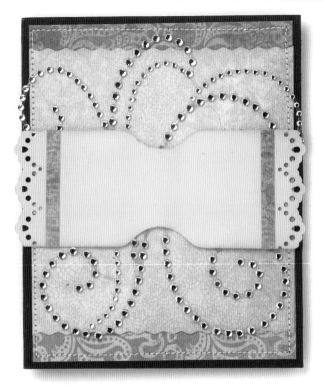

Mother's Day Flower Pin Card

By Lisa Dorsey

You can almost smell the roses on this beautiful Mother's Day card. Mom will be thrilled to know the beautiful felt rose on the front is also a pin she can wear proudly.

Materials List
cardstock: Bazzill Basics; *patterned paper:* My Mind's Eye; *gemstones:* Prima; *die:* Sizzix; *embossed felt:* Manufacturing Co.; *brads:* Creative Charms; *ink:* Ranger, Clearsnap; *punches:* EK Success, Martha Stewart; *pin back:* Darice

WHAT YOU'LL NEED

- ✪ Cardstock
- ✪ Paper trimmer
- ✪ Patterned paper
- ✪ Adhesive
- ✪ Decorative edged scissors
- ✪ Self-adhesive gem swirls
- ✪ Border punch
- ✪ Dies and die-cutting machine
- ✪ Embossed felt
- ✪ Ink pad
- ✪ Fabric glue
- ✪ Decorative brad or button
- ✪ Circle punch
- ✪ Hot glue
- ✪ Pin back
- ✪ Sewing machine and thread (optional)
- ✪ White gel pen (optional)

The Basics

1. Create a standard A2 card base from red cardstock (4¼" × 5½" [10.8cm × 14cm]).
2. Cut a piece of blue patterned paper to 4" × 5" (10.2cm × 12.7cm) and adhere it to the card.
3. Cut a piece of light blue patterned paper to 4" × 4½" (10.2cm × 11.4cm). Trim the 4" (10.2cm) sides of this piece with decorative edged scissors and adhere it to the card. Machine-stitch around the edges of the blue cardstock piece, if desired.
4. Adhere self-adhesive gem swirls to the card.
5. Cut a 1¾" × 4¾" (4.5cm × 12cm) strip of yellow cardstock. Border punch the short ends of the strip. Adhere two 1¾" × ¼" (4.5cm × 6mm) strips of blue patterned paper to the yellow cardstock as shown in the photo above. Adhere the yellow cardstock piece to the card.
6. Die cut embossed red felt with Sizzix flower dies. Ink the edges of the felt flowers. (See steps 4–6 on page 75.)
7. Adhere the flower pieces together with fabric glue. Adhere a decorative brad, button or other embellishment to the center of the flower and adhere the flower to the card.

Beyond the Basics

To Start:

Follow **The Basics**, steps 1–4. Do **The Basics** step 5, but do not adhere the cardstock to the base. Instead...

1 Create a place to attach the flower pin. Use a circle punch to create a half-circle notch on both sides of the center of the yellow cardstock strip, as shown.

2 Make sure the pin will fit around the notched area. Continue to trim the cardstock as needed.

3 Adhere the yellow cardstock piece to the card, adhering it on the ends and leaving the center unattached.

4 Create the flower pin by die cutting three large flowers, one medium flower and one small flower from red felt.

5 Attach the flowers together; thread as many as possible onto the brad. Don't worry if they can't all be threaded onto the brad.

6 Hot glue the remaining flowers to the back of the flowered brad.

7 Hot glue the flower to the pin back.

8 Attach the flower to the card.

Mother's Day Bookmark Card

By Lisa Dorsey

A vintage-inspired Mother's Day card is sure to please. Include a beautiful bookmark right on the front of the card for a nice little gift. She'll think of you every time she uses it!

The Basics

1. Create a 5" × 7⅛" (12.7cm × 18cm) card base from red cardstock.
2. Cut a piece of dark pink patterned paper to 4½" × 6⅞" (11.4cm × 17.5cm).
3. Cut a piece of light pink patterned paper to 4¼" × 6½" (10.8cm × 16.5cm) and adhere it to the piece of dark pink patterned paper.
4. Cut a piece of cream cardstock to 2½" × 4¼" (6.4cm × 10.8cm) and adhere it to the bottom of the light pink cardstock. Cut a piece of lace approximately 5" (12.7cm) long and adhere it to the area where the light pink and cream cardstocks meet. Machine-stitch around the edges of the light pink patterned paper, if desired.
5. Adhere the patterned paper and lace piece to the card base.
6. Print a vintage image onto white cardstock and die cut or hand cut it into a decorative label shape. Mat the image with red cardstock and adhere it to the card.
7. Cut a piece of red cardstock to 2" × 5¼" (5cm × 13.3cm) and adhere it to the card.
8. Cut a piece of floral patterned paper to 1¾" × 5" (4.5cm × 12.7cm) and adhere it to the red cardstock rectangle.
9. Embellish the card with flowers, buttons, ribbons and pearls.
10. Cut a strip of red cardstock to 1½" × ½" (3.8cm × 1.3cm), glue a small bow to the strip, and adhere the strip above the red cardstock rectangle for a finishing touch.

WHAT YOU'LL NEED

- ✪ Cardstock
- ✪ Paper trimmer
- ✪ Patterned paper
- ✪ Adhesive
- ✪ Lace
- ✪ Scissors
- ✪ Vintage image
- ✪ Paper flowers
- ✪ Buttons
- ✪ Ribbon
- ✪ Pearls
- ✪ White gel pen
- ✪ Craft knife
- ✪ Adhesive dots
- ✪ Sewing machine and thread (optional)

Beyond the Basics

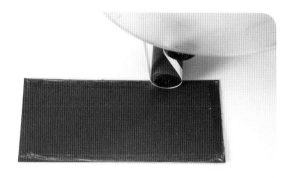

1 Create the card base and embellish it as instructed in **The Basics.** Create a pocket for the bookmark by cutting a piece of patterned paper to 2" × 5" (5cm × 12.7cm) and mat it with red cardstock. Add adhesive to all edges except the top edge.

2 Adhere the pocket to the front of the card.

3 Create a bookmark by cutting a piece of red cardstock to 1½" × 5½" (3.8cm × 14cm). Embellish the bookmark, and slide it into the pocket.

4 Using a white gel pen, faux stitch around three sides of the pocket.

Materials List *cardstock:* Bazzill Basics; *patterned paper:* The Paper Studio, My Mind's Eye, Crate Paper, Making Memories; *floral image:* Altered Bits; *die:* Sizzix; *punch:* EK Success; *pearls:* Creative Charms; *lace:* Jo-Ann Fabric and Craft Stores; *flower embellishments:* Prima; *ink:* Ranger; *buttons:* unknown; *adhesive dots:* Glue Dots International

Father's Day Baseball Penny Slider Card

By Kimber McGray

Play ball! Celebrate Father's Day with a card as cool as Dad is. This one will knock it out of the park!

WHAT YOU'LL NEED

- ✪ Card base
- ✪ Paper trimmer
- ✪ Cardstock
- ✪ Corner rounder
- ✪ Patterned paper
- ✪ Adhesive
- ✪ Border punch
- ✪ Twine
- ✪ Foam adhesive
- ✪ Stamp
- ✪ Ink
- ✪ Buttons
- ✪ Sewing machine and thread
- ✪ Circle punch
- ✪ Pencil
- ✪ Craft knife

Materials List *cardstock:* Bazzill Basics, Jillibean Soup; *patterned paper:* American Crafts, BoBunny Press; *stamps:* Papertrey Ink; *twine:* Jillibean Soup; *buttons:* Buttons Galore; *punches:* Stampin' Up!, EK Success

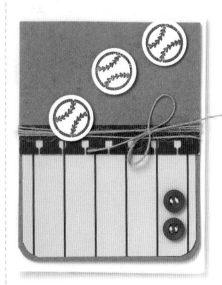

The Basics

1. Start with a standard A2 white card base (4¼" × 5½" [10.8cm × 14cm]).

2. Cut a piece of Kraft cardstock to 5" × 3¾" (12.7cm × 9.5cm), and round the bottom corners with a corner rounder.

3. Cut a piece of stripe-patterned paper 3½" × 2½" (9cm × 6.4cm), round the bottom corners with a corner rounder and adhere the piece to the Kraft cardstock.

4. Punch a 3¾" × ½" (9.5cm × 1.3cm) strip of red patterned paper with a border punch and adhere it to the Kraft cardstock.

5. Wrap twine around the Kraft cardstock and adhere it to the card with foam adhesive.

6. Add to the card baseballs that were stamped and punched using a circle punch. Finish embellishing the card by adhering a few buttons.

Beyond the Basics

The instructions for this card illustrate another way to make a penny slider card (see also pages 54 and 84), this one utilizing freehand drawing and cutting of the slider channel. Like the other penny slider instructions, you'll perform most of the steps listed under **The Basics** (you'll skip step 6), just with a few additions.

To Start:

Steps 1 and 2 below will come after **The Basics** step 2. Step 3 below will come after **The Basics** step 5.

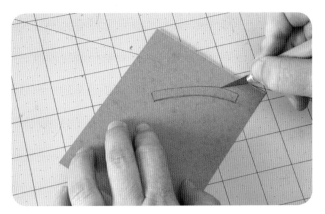

1 Start with a standard A2 white card base (4¼" × 5½" [10.8cm × 14cm]). Draw a path for the spinner on a 3¾" × 5" (9.5cm ×12.7cm) piece of Kraft cardstock with pencil (½" [1.3cm] wide). Cut out the path with a craft knife. Round the bottom corners with a corner rounder.

2 Layer the same color cardstock underneath, 3¾" × 5" (9.5cm × 12.7cm). Round the bottom corners. Adhere with foam squares. Embellish the front of the card with patterned paper and twine.

3 Create the penny slider by adhering two pennies together with a small foam square and embellishing with a stamped baseball image. Insert the slider in the slider channel. Adhere this panel to the front of the card base.

Father's Day Fishing Fancy Fold Card

By Kimber McGray

Be one with the water and enjoy a peaceful day of fishing. Simulate this feeling with a Father's Day card any angler would be happy to reel in.

Materials List *cardstock:* Core'dinations, Jillibean Soup; *punch:* EK Success; *metal embellishments:* The Paper Studio; *floss:* DMC

The Basics

1. Create a 3" × 6" (7.6cm × 15.2cm) card base from blue cardstock.

2. Cut a piece of Kraft cardstock to 2¾" × 5" (7cm × 12.7cm) and adhere it to the front of the card.

3. Cut a strip of blue cardstock to 1" × 12½" (2.5cm × 31.8cm). Using a circle punch, punch "waves" along one edge of the strip. Sand the edges of the strip with a sanding block or sandpaper.

4. Cut the strip into four 2 ½" (6.4cm) long pieces. Layer the pieces and adhere the pieces to one another, and then adhere that piece to the Kraft cardstock.

5. Embellish the card with fishing stickers or chipboard pieces and a floss fishing line.

Beyond the Basics

1 Cut a piece of blue cardstock to 11" × 6" (28cm × 15.2cm) and score the cardstock, from the left, at 2¾", 5½" and 8¼" (7cm, 14cm and 21cm).

2 Cut a triangle off the cardstock, as shown, starting approximately 2" (5cm) up from the bottom left corner and continuing to approximately 2" (5cm) from the top right corner.

3 Use a 1" (2.5cm) circle punch to create waves along the cut edge.

4 Using a sanding block, sand the edges of the cardstock.

5 Fold along the score lines to create the card. Embellish the card with fishing rod and lure embellishments. Add a piece of embroidery floss from the fishing rod to the lures, as shown in the photo on page 80, to complete the card.

Halloween Honeycomb Pumpkin Card

By Kimber McGray

Two fun crafty products make this Halloween card great spooky fun. Chalkboard cardstock allows you to set a spooky scene or write out an eerie message, and a honeycomb paper pumpkin brightens the scene.

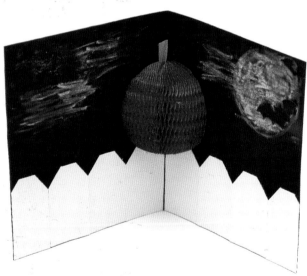

Materials List *cardstock:* Core'dinations; Chalkstock: Canvas Corp; *honeycomb paper:* Inky Antics; *punches:* Stampin' Up!, Martha Stewart, EK Success; *stickers:* Making Memories; *pen:* Uni-Ball Signo; *chalk:* Crayola

The Basics

1. Cut a piece of cardstock to 4" × 9" (10.2cm × 23cm) and fold it in half to create a 4" × 4½" (10.2cm × 11.4cm) card base.
2. Cut a strip of white cardstock to 1¼" × 4" (3.2cm × 10.2cm) and clip one end off at a diagonal. Adhere the strip to the card.
3. Cut a strip of orange cardstock to ½" × 3½" (1.3cm × 9cm) and clip one end off at a diagonal. Adhere this strip to the white cardstock strip.
4. Cut a piece of chalkboard cardstock to 3" × 2" (7.6cm × 5cm). Punch the corners with a ticket punch. With a white gel pen, outline ¼" (6mm) from the edges of the chalkboard cardstock. Adhere the chalkboard cardstock piece to the card, over the white and orange cardstock strips.
5. Embellish with dimensional stickers or write a sentiment on the chalkboard cardstock with a piece of chalk.

- Cardstock
- Paper trimmer
- Adhesive
- Chalkboard cardstock
- Tag punch
- White gel pen
- Dimensional stickers
- Chalk
- Pencil
- Scissors
- Honeycomb paper

Beyond the Basics

To Start:

Create the card front as directed in **The Basics.** Adhere a 4" × 9" (10.2cm × 23cm) piece of chalkboard cardstock to the interior of the card. Cut eight pieces of white cardstock to 1" × 1¾" (2.5cm × 4.5cm). Snip off the corners as shown in the photo on page 82 (or, use a tag punch to make the fence picket). Then...

1 Draw a half circle on a piece of orange honeycomb paper, following the manufacturer's instructions.

2 Cut the half circle from the honeycomb paper.

3 Adhere one side of the honeycomb paper circle to the interior of the card, lining it up with the center fold.

4 Adhere the other side of the honeycomb paper to the interior of the card.

5 Draw a spooky scene with chalk on the chalkboard cardstock. Adhere a bat punched from black cardstock in front of a hand-drawn full moon. To create the fence, adhere the picket pieces along the bottom edge of the interior of the card.

Halloween Spider Spinner Card

By Nichol Magouirk

No need to worry about frightening your friends with this silly Halloween spider card! The googly eyes will leave them laughing. The spider gets even sillier as he spins across the stamped web when you step it up and create a penny spinner card.

The Basics

1. Start with a standard A2 card base (5½" × 4¼" [14cm × 10.8cm]) in white.

2. Cut a piece of black cardstock to 5¼" × 4" (13.3cm × 10.2cm), and, using white ink, stamp the black cardstock piece with a spider-web patterned stamp. Round the top corners of the cardstock with a ½" (1.3cm) corner rounder.

3. Cut a strip of vellum to 1" × 5¼" (2.5cm × 13.3cm) and score the vellum ⅛" (3mm) from the top and bottom edges using a bone folder.

4. Adhere orange twill tape to the top of the card. Layer the vellum over the twill tape and staple it in place.

5. Thread string through a button and adhere the button to the vellum strip.

6. Stamp a moon using yellow ink. Faux stitch the moon with a white gel pen.

7. Stamp two bats and a spider on white cardstock with black

ink and color the images with markers. Cut out the bats and use a 1" (2.5cm) circle punch to punch out the spider.

8. Punch a 1¼" (3.2cm) circle from gray cardstock. Adhere the spider circle to the gray circle.

9. Punch a 1½" (3.8cm) scalloped circle from orange cardstock and adhere the matted spider circle to it. Glue googly eyes to the spider and adhere the spider to the card with foam adhesive.

10. Add gemstones to the bottom right corner of the card.

Materials List *card base:* Hero Arts; *cardstock:* Papertrey Ink, Neenah; *vellum:* The Paper Studio; *stamps:* Hero Arts, Lawn Fawn, Papertrey Ink; *ink:* Memento by Tsukineko, Stampin' Up!, ColorBox; *markers:* Copic; *pen:* Uni-Ball Signo; *button:* Doodlebug Designs; *eyes:* Hobby Lobby; *stapler:* Tim Holtz; *twill:* Papertrey Ink; *gemstones:* Hero Arts; *scoring board:* Martha Stewart; *die-cutting machine:* Silhouette America; *punches:* EK Success, The Paper Studio, We R Memory Keepers

- ✪ Card base
- ✪ Paper trimmer
- ✪ Cardstock
- ✪ Ink
- ✪ Stamps
- ✪ Corner rounder
- ✪ Vellum
- ✪ Bone folder
- ✪ Twill tape
- ✪ Stapler
- ✪ Button
- ✪ String
- ✪ Adhesive
- ✪ White gel pen
- ✪ Markers
- ✪ Craft knife
- ✪ Circle punch
- ✪ Googly eyes
- ✪ Foam adhesive
- ✪ Gemstones
- ✪ Die-cutting machine
- ✪ Pennies

Beyond the Basics

To Start:

For the penny slider version of this card, you will follow all of the steps in **The Basics,** but with a few additions.

You will do step 1 below after you cut out the black cardstock, but before you stamp the cardstock.

You'll do step 2 below after **The Basics** step 2 or 3 but before **The Basics** step 4.

You'll do steps 3 and 4 below after **The Basics** step 9.

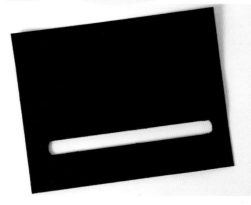

1 Using Silhouette software, create a slider channel in the black cardstock piece. The penny slider opening needs to be just a bit larger than the width of the foam adhesive but smaller than a penny. This will allow the slider to move freely while preventing the penny from falling out of the slot.

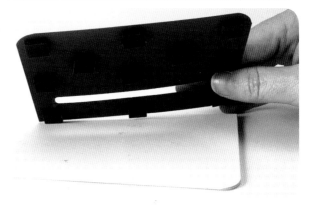

2 After embellishing the front of the cardstock, adhere it to the front of the card base with foam adhesive.

3 Create a penny slider by adhering two pennies together with foam adhesive.

4 Slide the penny piece into the slider channel. Embellish the top penny piece with a stamped spider. Adhere googly eyes to the stamped spider.

Celebrations

THERE ARE SO MANY different things to celebrate in life: traveling life's journey with our friends and family, showing our support and offering our congratulations. Doing these things lets loved ones know we care and support them in all of their endeavors.

In this chapter, we will help you celebrate the milestones in the lives of your loved ones. Imagine the pride your favorite new driver will feel when he receives the cool, interactive scooter card. For graduates, we have a great congratulatory card that tosses a mortarboard in the air right alongside them.

You can also help a bride and groom celebrate their nuptials with an amazing three-tiered wedding cake that extends to reveal a gift card.

Or maybe you know someone who is moving into a new home. We have cards for that occasion too.

And then there are new babies. Learn how to make an adorable card that opens to reveal a sweet hanging mobile—perfect for your friend's baby boy or girl.

And surely you know someone approaching a significant anniversary. Our cards honoring 25th and 50th anniversaries will dazzle with the sparkle, glitz and, most of all, the love you put into them!

Wedding Cake Card and Gift Card Holder

By Kimber McGray

A simple wedding card adorned with a sweet cake is a great way to congratulate the newlyweds on their big day. Now imagine their awe when you hand them a card that extends to an amazing three-tiered cake that includes a gift card to their favorite store. Either way, they will enjoy this sweet treat of a handmade card.

WHAT YOU'LL NEED

- ✪ Cardstock
- ✪ Paper trimmer
- ✪ Sewing machine and thread
- ✪ Corner, border, circle and hole punches
- ✪ Sandpaper
- ✪ Adhesive
- ✪ Ribbon
- ✪ Chipboard embellishments
- ✪ Self-adhesive pearls
- ✪ Foam adhesive
- ✪ Bone folder
- ✪ Craft knife
- ✪ Brads
- ✪ Adhesive dots

Materials List *cardstock:* Core'dinations; *chipboard:* Momenta; *ribbon:* Creative Impressions; *pearls:* Queen & Co.; *punch:* Fiskars; *adhesive dots:* Glue Dots International

The Basics

1. Start with a basic white card base in a standard A2 size (4¼" × 5½" [10.8cm × 14cm]).

2. Machine stitch a border ¼" (6mm) from all edges.

3. Cut three pieces of gray cardstock to: 3½" × 2" (9cm × 5cm), 3¼" × 1½" (8.3cm × 3.8cm) and 2¾" × 1½" (7cm × 3.8cm). Round the top corners and lightly sand the edges of all three pieces. Adhere the pieces together, layering them to create a cake shape.

4. Cut a strip from white cardstock to 3¼" × ½" (8.3cm × 1.3cm) and scallop the edge with a scalloped border punch. Adhere the strip to the middle tier of the cake and trim the edges.

5. Wrap a ribbon around the bottom layer and tie it into a bow.

6. Adhere chipboard flowers and pearls to the cake for decoration.

7. Adhere the embellished cake to the card base with foam adhesive.

Beyond the Basics

1 Cut three pieces of gray cardstock to 11" × 3½" (28cm × 9cm), 8½" × 3¼" (21.6cm × 8.3cm) and 6" × 2¾" (15.2cm × 7cm). From the left, score the large piece at ½" (1.3cm) and 5¾" (14.6cm), the medium piece at ½" (1.3cm) and 4½" (11.4cm) and the small piece at ½" (1.3cm) and 3¼" (8.3cm).

2 *On the middle panel of the large piece:* Using a craft knife, cut a 1" (2.5cm) slot, 2½" (6.4cm) from the bottom, on each score line. (In a later step, ribbon will be inserted through these slots.)

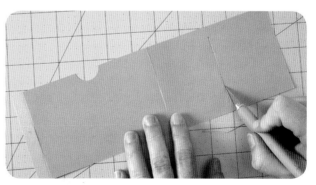

3 *On the middle panel of the large piece:* Punch a ½" (1.3cm) circle notch in the center of the top edge with a 1" (2.5cm) punch.

4 *On the end panel of the large piece:* Cut a ⁄₁₆" (1.5mm) channel in the middle of the panel, starting ½" (1.3cm) from the top edge and ending ½" (1.3cm) from the bottom edge.

5 *On the large piece:* Fold in on the ½" (1.3cm) score line to form a tab and adhere the tab to the cardstock to close this tier or pocket.

6 *On the middle panel of the medium piece:* Punch a ½" (1.3cm) circle notch in the center of the top edge with a 1" (2.5cm) punch.

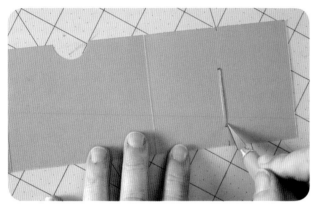

7 *On the end panel of the medium piece:* Cut a ¹⁄₁₆" (1.5mm) channel in the middle of the panel, starting ½" (1.3cm) from the top edge and ending ½" (1.3cm) from the bottom edge.

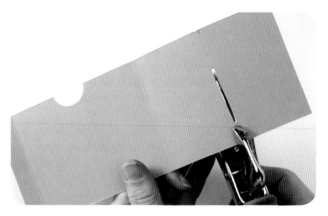

8 *On the end panel of the medium piece:* Punch a small hole in the bottom of the panel, ¼" (6mm) from the bottom and centered.

9 *On the medium piece:* Fold in on the ½" (1.3cm) score line to form a tab and adhere the tab to the cardstock to close this tier or pocket.

10 *On the end panel of the small piece:* Punch a small hole in the bottom of the panel, ¼" (6mm) from the bottom and centered.

11 *On the small piece:* Fold in on the ½" (1.3cm) score line to form a tab and adhere the tab to the cardstock to close this tier or pocket.

12 *To assemble the card:* Insert the medium piece into the large piece.

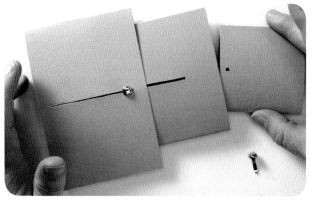

13 Line up the channels and insert a brad into the channel in the large piece and through the hole in the medium piece.

14 Extend the medium piece and insert the small piece into the medium piece.

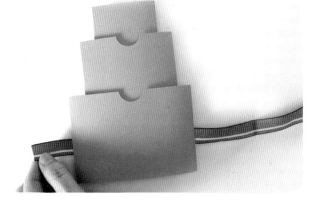

15 Line up the hole in the small piece with the channel in the medium piece and insert a brad to attach the tiers.

16 With all pieces extended, slide a ribbon through the slits in the bottom tier, bring the ribbon to the front and tie it in a bow. Finish embellishing the front of the card with border-punched white cardstock, chipboard flowers and self-adhesive pearls.

Baby Mobile Pop-Up Card

By Kimber McGray

Does someone have a new baby? This adorable and whimsical mobile pop-up card will warm the hearts of any new parents as you congratulate them on their little bundle of joy.

WHAT YOU'LL NEED

- ✪ Cardstock
- ✪ Paper trimmer
- ✪ Patterned paper
- ✪ Adhesive
- ✪ Hole, star and border punches
- ✪ Corner rounder
- ✪ Buttons
- ✪ Pencil
- ✪ Craft knife
- ✪ Baby-themed embellishments
- ✪ Embroidery floss

Materials List *cardstock:* Core'dinations; *patterned paper:* Jillibean Soup; *felt embellishments:* KI Memories; *punches:* Fiskars, Stampin' Up!; *buttons:* Stampin' Up!; *floss:* DMC

The Basics

1. Create a standard A2 card base (4¼" × 5½" [10.8cm × 14cm]) from white cardstock.
2. Cut a piece of patterned paper to 4" × 5¼" (10.2cm × 13.3cm) and adhere it to the card.
3. Scallop one edge of a 1" × 4" (2.5cm × 10.2cm) strip of white cardstock and adhere it to the top of the card front.
4. Cut a piece of white cardstock to 1" × 1½" (2.5cm × 3.8cm), round two of the corners of the piece and adhere the piece to the bottom right corner of the card.
5. Embellish the card with a star punched from blue cardstock and a few buttons.

Beyond the Basics

To Start:

Make the front of the card according to the instructions for **The Basics.** Then...

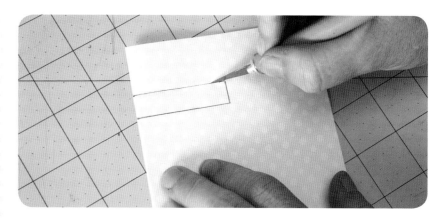

1 Cut a piece of patterned paper to ¼" × 8¼" (6mm × 21cm) and fold it in half. This will be your card liner. On the folded edge, draw a box, marking the paper at 1" (2.5cm) and 1½" (3.8cm) from the top. You'll want the strip to be 2" (5cm) long. Unfold the lining and cut along the long sides of the box only.

2 Adhere a piece of white cardstock cut to ½" × 4" (1.3cm × 10.2cm) over the pop-up strip.

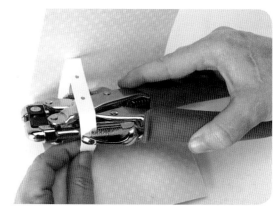

3 Punch holes in the white strip.

4 Adhere the card liner to the interior of the card base.

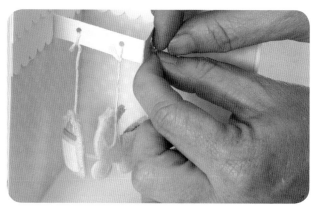

5 Tie baby-themed embellishments through the holes in the pop-up strip. Finish embellishing the inside of the card by adding strips of scallop-punched paper to the top edge of the card.

New Home Gift Card Holder

By Kelly Goree

Moving into a new home is very exciting. Send a fun, customized card to congratulate the homeowner. The fancy version of this one holds a gift card. Don't forget to embellish the front door, windows and flower boxes of the house!

The Basics

1. Create a 4½" × 4½" (11.4cm × 11.4cm) card base out of white cardstock.

2. Cut a piece of stripe-patterned paper to 4½" × 4½" (11.4cm × 11.4cm) and adhere it to the card.

3. Using the template on page 136, cut a roof shape out of brown patterned paper. Scallop the bottom edge of the roof and adhere it to the card, aligning the top edge of the roof to the top edge of the card.

4. Cut a piece of white cardstock to 1½" × 2⅛" (3.8cm × 5.4cm). Cut a 1¼" × 2" (3.2cm × 5cm) piece of yellow patterned paper. Adhere the yellow paper to the white cardstock and adhere this piece to the card.

5. Punch a 4½" × ½" (11.4cm × 1.3cm) strip of green cardstock with a decorative border punch and adhere it to the bottom edge of the card.

6. Create the windows by cutting two ¾" × 1¾" (2cm × 4.5cm) pieces and one ¾" × ¾" (2cm × 2cm) piece of blue patterned paper.

7. Mat the windows with white cardstock and trim so just a little bit of a white edge shows as a border around the windows.

8. Adhere the larger windows to either side of the door. Set the smaller window aside.

9. Adhere a small 1⅛" × ⅛" (3cm × 3mm) strip of white cardstock to the top of each of the two larger windows.

10. Adhere a 1⅛" × ½" (3cm × 1.3cm) piece of white cardstock to the bottom of the larger windows to create flower boxes.

11. Cut a piece of stripe-patterned paper to 1½" × 1¾" (3.8cm × 4.5cm). Trim one end into a triangular shape and adhere it to the roof with foam adhesive. Adhere the ¾" × ¾" (2cm × 2cm) blue window to the patterned paper square.

12. Scallop a 3" × ¼" (7.6cm × 6mm) strip of white cardstock, cut it in half and adhere it above the roof window.

13. Embellish the card with markers, Glossy Accents, brads and more, as desired.

(See the basic card on page 86.)

Materials List

cardstock: Bazzill Basics; *patterned paper:* BoBunny Press; *stickers:* BasicGrey; *brad:* BasicGrey; *glossy medium:* Ranger Glossy Accents; *pen:* Zig and Uni-Ball Signo; *punch:* Fiskars

94

Beyond the Basics

WHAT YOU'LL NEED

- ✪ Cardstock
- ✪ Paper trimmer
- ✪ Patterned paper
- ✪ Pencil
- ✪ Craft knife
- ✪ Border punch
- ✪ Adhesive
- ✪ Foam adhesive
- ✪ Border punch
- ✪ Markers
- ✪ Glossy Accents
- ✪ Decorative brads

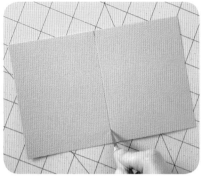

1 Use the template on page 136 to make the card base out of cardstock. Using a craft knife, cut a slit along the fold, leaving ¼" (6mm) uncut at each edge.

2 Use the template on page 136 to cut a slider out of cardstock.

3 Slide the "T" through the slit in the card base so the "T" is inside the card, as shown.

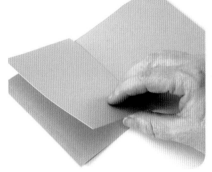

4 Adhere the edges of the card, encasing the "T" inside and securing this sliding mechanism in place.

5 Using the template on page 136, cut a roof shape out of cardstock.

6 Adhere the free end of the sliding mechanism inside the roof. Pulling on the roof should pull the slider up from the card base.

7 Pull the slider up from the base and lay a gift card on the panel. With a pencil, mark slots in which to insert the card corners.

8 Use a craft knife to cut the slots. Embellish the card following instructions for **The Basics**.

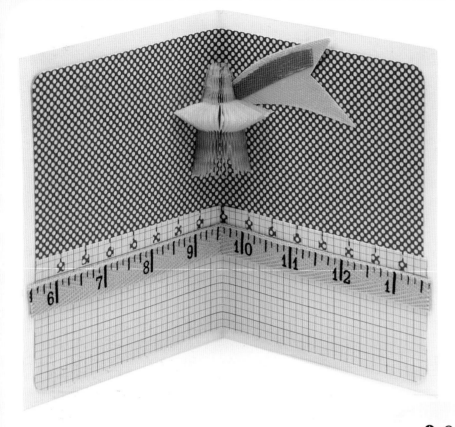

Congrats Honeycomb Stars Card

By Kimber McGray

Recognizing the achievements of a child is so very important. Encourage them to reach for the stars and let them know anything can be accomplished.

WHAT YOU'LL NEED

- Cardstock
- Paper trimmer
- Patterned paper
- Adhesive
- Border and star punches
- Corner rounder
- Twill tape
- Metal ring
- Foam adhesive
- Pencil
- Scissors
- Honeycomb paper

Materials List *cardstock:* Core'dinations; *patterned paper:* Jillibean Soup, My Mind's Eye; *ribbon:* Jillibean Soup; *tag:* Avery; *punches:* Stampin' Up!, Fiskars, EK Success; *honeycomb paper:* Inky Antics; *foam adhesive squares:* 3L Scrapbook Adhesives

The Basics

1. Create a standard A2 card base (4¼" × 5½" [10.8cm × 14cm]) from white cardstock.
2. Cut a piece of blue patterned paper to 3¾" × 5" (9.5cm × 12.7cm) and adhere it to the front of the card.
3. Cut a piece of grid patterned paper to 3¾" × 2¼" (9.5cm × 5.7cm). Punch the top edge with a border punch and round the bottom edges with a corner rounder. Adhere the piece to the card, aligning it with the bottom edge of the blue patterned paper piece.
4. Adhere a 3¾" (9.5cm) piece of decorative twill tape to the card.
5. Adhere a metal ring tag to the card with foam adhesive.
6. Punch a star out of yellow cardstock. Cut the star tails from yellow and orange cardstock, using the templates on page 136. Adhere the tails to the back of the star.
7. Adhere the star to the metal ring tag, and adhere the metal ring tag to the card with foam adhesive.

Beyond the Basics

To Start:

Follow all **The Basics** steps to create the card front. Cut a piece of blue patterned paper to 8" × 3½" (20.3cm × 9cm). Round corners with a corner rounder and adhere the paper to the interior of the card. Cut a piece of grid-patterned paper to 8" × 2" (20cm × 5cm). Use a border punch on the top edge of the paper and round the bottom corners. Adhere it to the interior of the card. Adhere an 8" (20cm) piece of printed twill over the area where the two papers meet. Then...

1 Punch a star out of scrap paper. Cut it in half. Trace around the half star onto a piece of honeycomb paper, following the manufacturer's instructions.

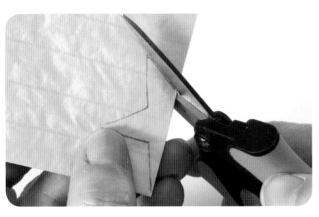

2 Cut the half star from the honeycomb paper.

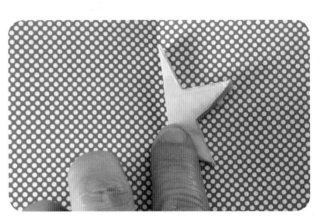

3 Adhere one side of the honeycomb star to the interior of card, along the center fold.

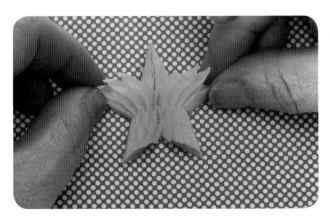

4 Adhere the other side of the honeycomb star to the card.

25th Anniversary Flip Card

By Kimber McGray

Congratulate the happy couple on twenty-five years of marriage with this beautiful interactive card embellished with tokens representative of their special day those many years ago.

WHAT YOU'LL NEED

- ✪ Cardstock
- ✪ Paper trimmer
- ✪ Patterned paper
- ✪ Adhesive
- ✪ Foam adhesive
- ✪ Dies and die-cutting machine
- ✪ Ring embellishment
- ✪ Brad
- ✪ Gems
- ✪ Bone folder
- ✪ Pencil
- ✪ Craft knife

Materials List *cardstock:* Core'dinations; *patterned paper:* Making Memories; *gems:* Queen & Co.; *metal rings:* Making Memories; *die:* QuicKutz; *punch:* Marvy Uchida, EK Success; *foam adhesive squares:* 3L Scrapbook Adhesives

The Basics

1. Create a standard A2 card base (4¼" × 5½" [10.8cm × 14cm]) from silver cardstock.
2. Cut a piece of stripe-patterned paper to 3¾" × 5" (9.5cm × 12.7cm) and adhere it to the card.
3. Cut a piece of white cardstock to 3" × 4" (7.6cm × 10.2cm) and adhere it to the card with foam adhesive.
4. Cut a piece of eyelet paper to 3" × 4" (7.6cm × 10.2cm) and adhere it over the white cardstock piece.
5. Die cut a 3" (7.6cm) heart from silver cardstock and a 2¾" (7cm) heart from white cardstock. Adhere the two together.
6. Die cut the number 25 from silver cardstock and adhere it to the front of the heart with foam adhesive.
7. Attach a ring embellishment to the heart with a brad. Cover the brad with a clear heart-shaped gemstone. Adhere the heart to the card with foam adhesive.

Beyond the Basics

1 Cut a piece of silver cardstock to 5½" × 6¼" (14cm × 16cm). From the left side of the cardstock, score at 2½" and 3½" (6.4cm and 9cm).

2 Using a pencil, draw lines 1" (2.5cm) from the top and bottom edges and 1½" (3.8cm) from the right and left edges (leaving 1" [2.5cm] in center). You'll have a 3" × 3½" 7.6cm × 9cm) rectangle in the middle of the card (leaving 1" [2.5cm] in center). With a craft knife, cut along all pencil lines except the lines that intersect the center 1" (2.5cm) fold.

3 Fold along the score lines in opposite directions to create the flip panel.

4 Cut two pieces of cardstock to 3" × 3½" (7.6xcm × 9cm), and adhere the pieces to the front and back of the flip panel. Embellish the card as directed in **The Basics.**

(View of the back of the card)

Baby Girl Fancy Fold Card

By Kimber McGray

Sugar and spice and everything nice! This beautiful embossed card is a wonderful way to congratulate the happy parents and welcome a new little one into this world.

Materials List *cardstock:* Core'dinations; *patterned paper:* BasicGrey; *punches:* Stampin' Up!, Marvy Uchida; *foam stickers:* Jolee's

WHAT YOU'LL NEED

- ✪ Cardstock
- ✪ Paper trimmer
- ✪ Adhesive
- ✪ Border and heart punches
- ✪ Sandpaper
- ✪ Foam adhesive
- ✪ Baby girl-themed embellishments
- ✪ Bone folder

The Basics

1. Create a standard A2 card base 4¼" × 5½" [10.8cm × 14cm]) from white cardstock.
2. Scallop the right edge of the card base with a border punch or decorative scissors.
3. Cut a 4" × 5½" (10.2cm × 14cm) piece of embossed cardstock. Lightly sand the cardstock and adhere it to the card.
4. Punch a heart from a piece of white cardstock and adhere it to the card with foam adhesive.
5. Adhere baby girl-themed embellishments to the heart.

Beyond the Basics

1 Cut a piece of pink cardstock to 5½" × 10¼" (14cm × 26cm). From the left, score the cardstock at 1½", 3", 4½" and 6" (3.8cm, 7.6cm, 11.4cm and 15.2cm).

2 Fold along the score lines to create an accordion fold.

3 Cut two pieces of white cardstock to 1¾" × 5½" (4.5cm × 14cm). Punch one 5½" (14cm) edge of each of the pieces with a scallop punch or trim with decorative-edge scissors. Adhere the strips to the inside edges of the first two accordion folds.

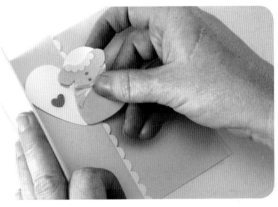

4 Punch a few hearts from white cardstock and embellish the hearts with baby girl-themed stickers. Adhere the hearts inside the accordion folds and on the back panel.

Graduation Pop-Up Card

By Kimber McGray

Spread the joy and pride in graduation! A light tug on the sides of this fancy card releases a mortarboard into the air. Make it extra special by customizing the card in the colors of your favorite grad's alma mater.

The Basics

1. Create a standard A2 card base (5½" × 4¼" [14cm × 10.8cm]) from white cardstock.
2. Hand draw an arc on a piece of 5½" (14cm) wide blue cardstock. Cut out the arc and mat it with yellow cardstock. Adhere the piece to the card.
3. Embellish the card with stars punched from yellow cardstock and graduation-themed embellishments.

WHAT YOU'LL NEED

- ✪ Cardstock
- ✪ Paper trimmer
- ✪ Pencil
- ✪ Craft knife
- ✪ Adhesive
- ✪ Star punch
- ✪ Graduation-themed embellishments
- ✪ Bone folder

Materials List *cardstock:* Core'dinations; *chipboard:* Momenta; *ribbon:* Creative Impressions; *pearls:* Queen & Co.; *punch:* Fiskars

Beyond the Basics

1 Cut two pieces of cardstock to 4¼" × 7" (10.8cm × 17.8cm). From the left, score at 1" and 2" (2.5cm and 5cm), and fold along the score lines.

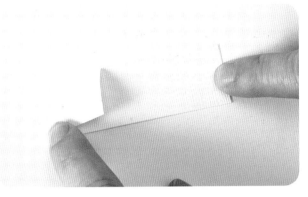

2 Create the pop-up piece: Cut a strip of cardstock to 1" × 3" (2.5cm × 7.6cm). Fold a 1" (2.5cm) triangle on one end of the strip to create a flap.

3 Adhere the flap to the second fold on one of the pieces of cardstock, about ½" (1.3cm) from the top edge of the cardstock.

4 Adhere the front and back pieces together, as shown.

5 Adhere graduation-themed embellishments to the pop-up piece. Embellish the front of the card according to **The Basics.**

New Home Accordion Fold Card

By Kimber McGray

Customize the house on this card to resemble the new home of your friend or family member. Then set the scene by tucking trees, grass and that happy home inside the valleys of a fun accordion-fold card.

Materials List *cardstock:* Jillibean Soup; *patterned paper:* Jillibean Soup; *corrugated shapes:* Jillibean Soup; *ink:* Maya Road; *punch:* EK Success

WHAT YOU'LL NEED

- ✪ Cardstock
- ✪ Paper trimmer
- ✪ Patterned paper
- ✪ Corner rounder
- ✪ Adhesive
- ✪ Craft knife
- ✪ Die-cut shapes
- ✪ Ink pads
- ✪ Foam adhesive
- ✪ Circle punch
- ✪ Bone folder

The Basics

1. Create a standard A2 card base (4¼" × 5½" [10.8cm × 14cm]) from Kraft cardstock.
2. Cut a piece of blue patterned paper to 4" × 4" (10.2cm × 10.2cm), round the top corners of the piece and adhere it to the card base.
3. Cut a piece of green patterned paper to 4" × 2½" (10.2cm × 6.4cm), fringe the top edge to create grass and adhere it to the card.
4. Cut a piece of yellow patterned paper to a size slightly smaller than the corrugated die-cut house. Pop the windows and door out of the house shape and then adhere the yellow paper to the back of the house.
5. Ink the front door with red ink and adhere it back in place. Adhere the house on the front of the card with foam adhesive.
6. Hand cut a Kraft paper sidewalk and adhere it to the card front, from the door to the bottom edge of the card.
7. Punch a 1½" (3.8cm) circle from green patterned Kraft paper. Adhere a die-cut tree trunk onto the front of the circle and adhere the tree to the card with foam adhesive.

Beyond the Basics

1 Cut a piece of Kraft cardstock to 5½" × 11½" (14cm × 29.2cm). From the left, score at 4¼", 4¾", 5¼", 5¾", 6¼", 6¾" and 7¼" (10.8cm, 12cm, 13.3cm, 14.6cm, 16cm, 17.2cm and 18.4cm).

2 Fold along the score lines to create a 5½" × 4¼" (14cm × 10.8cm) card base.

3 On the ends only, adhere the folds together.

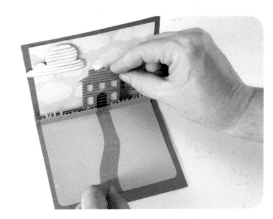

4 Embellish the interior of the card with patterned paper and adhere embellishments in the valleys of the accordion folds.

To Finish:

The front of the card can be embellished with patterned papers (skies and grass, for example) and more.

New Wheels Scooter Pull Card

By Kimber McGray

Vroom vroom … gentlemen, start your engines! Celebrate the coming-of-age ritual of getting your first set of wheels or earning your driver's license with this delightful slider card.

WHAT YOU'LL NEED

- ✪ Cardstock
- ✪ Paper trimmer
- ✪ Stamps
- ✪ Ink pads
- ✪ White gel pen
- ✪ Adhesive
- ✪ Ruler
- ✪ Markers
- ✪ Craft knife
- ✪ Foam adhesive
- ✪ Bone folder
- ✪ Pencil
- ✪ Corner rounder

Materials List *cardstock:* Core'dinations; *stamps:* Paper Smooches, Jillibean Soup; *ink:* Momento by Tsukineko; *markers:* Copic; *pen:* Uni-Ball Signo; *foam adhesive squares:* 3L Scrapbook Adhesives

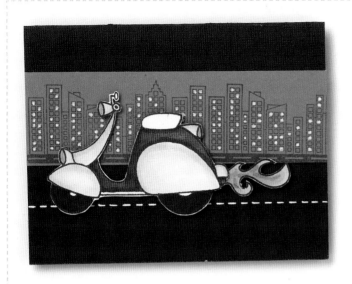

The Basics

1. Create a standard A2 card base (4¼" × 5½" [10.8cm × 14cm]) from black cardstock.

2. Cut a 2" × 5½" (5cm × 14cm) strip of gray cardstock. Stamp a city image with black ink and color in random windows with a white gel pen. Adhere this strip to the card.

3. Using a ruler, draw dashed lines with a white gel pen on the black card to create street markings.

4. Using the template on page 138, cut out one scooter on white cardstock, color it with markers and cut it out. Adhere the scooter to the card with foam adhesive.

Beyond the Basics

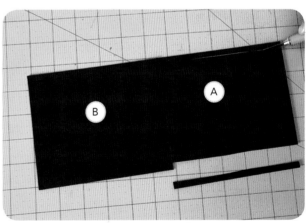

1 Create a standard A2 card base (4¼" × 5½" [10.8cm × 14cm]) from black cardstock and set it aside. Then cut a piece of black cardstock to 4¾" × 11¼" (12cm × 28.6cm). Score at ¼" (6mm) along both long sides and one short side. Score at 5½" (14cm) from the unscored short side.

2 Trim off the ¼" (6mm) scored piece from Panel A with a craft knife.

3 Trim off the corners from Panel B with a craft knife.

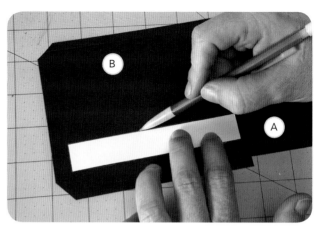

4 Create a rectangle template measuring ¾" × 5" (2cm × 12.7cm). Place the template on panel B, ½" (1.3cm) from the bottom edge and centered. Trace around the template with a pencil.

5 Using a craft knife, cut out the rectangle.

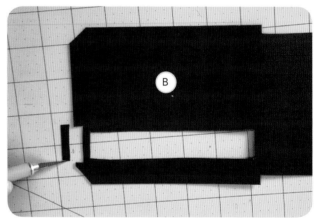

6 Using a craft knife, cut out a 1" (2.5cm) notch from the left edge, next to the rectangular opening for the slide pull.

7 Create the slide from a 4" × 5¾" (10.2cm × 14.6cm) piece of black cardstock. The stop on the left is 1" (2.5cm) wide and the slide is 1" (2.5cm) wide. Cut ¼" (6mm) off the bottom and 2¾" (7cm) off the top.

8 Round the corners of the slide with a corner rounder.

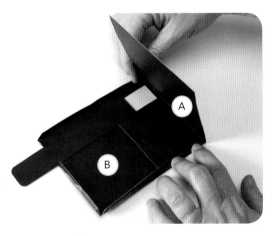

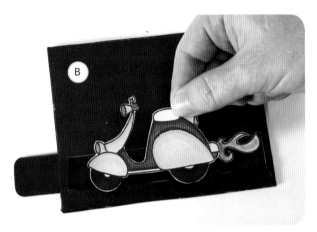

9 Fold up all scored pieces and add adhesive to the ¼" (6mm) tabs. Lay the slide in the notch. Adhere closed.

10 Using the template on page 138, cut out one scooter on white cardstock, color it with markers and cut it out. Adhere the scooter to the slide with foam adhesive.

To Finish:
Adhere the slider portion of the card to the card base. Embellish the card following steps 2 and 4 of **The Basics.** Using a ruler and a white gel pen, draw dashed lines on the slide and behind the slide.

50th Anniversary Sizzix Pop-Up Card

By Kimber McGray

A golden anniversary is something to celebrate! This beautiful card honors the happy couple on their grand achievement.

WHAT YOU'LL NEED

- Cardstock
- Paper trimmer
- Heart, border and hole punches
- Sewing machine and thread
- Adhesive
- Ribbon
- Foam adhesive
- Dies and die-cutting machine

Materials List *cardstock:* Core'dinations; *ribbon:* Creative Impressions; *punches:* Stampin' Up!, Creative Memories; *dies:* Sizzix and QuicKutz; *foam adhesive squares:* 3L Scrapbook Adhesives

The Basics

1. Create a standard A2 card base (4¼" × 5½" [10.8cm × 14cm]) from white shimmer cardstock.

2. Cut a piece of pink shimmer cardstock to 3¾" × 5" (9.5cm × 12.7cm).

3. Cut two pieces of white shimmer cardstock to 2" × 5" (5cm × 12.7cm) and two pieces of red shimmer cardstock to 1½" × 5" (3.8cm × 12.7cm). Scallop one 5" (13cm) edge of each piece of red shimmer cardstock.

4. Lay the white shimmer pieces on the pink shimmer piece; then lay the red shimmer pieces on the white shimmer pieces. Machine stitch across the top edge of each red shimmer piece, sewing through all three layers. Adhere the pink shimmer piece to the card base.

5. Cut a 2½" × 4" (6.4cm × 10.2cm) piece of white shimmer cardstock and trim the corners to create a tag. Punch a small hole in the top of the tag. Tie a ribbon through the hole and adhere the tag to the card with foam adhesive.

6. Die cut the number 50 from gold glitter cardstock and adhere it to the tag with foam adhesive.

7. Punch two sets of hearts from red and pink shimmer cardstock. Adhere the hearts to each other as shown in the photo above, and adhere the hearts to the tag with foam adhesive.

Beyond the Basics

To Start:
Follow steps 1–4 of **The Basics.** Then...

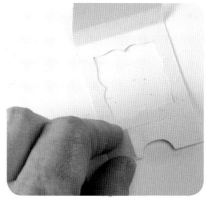

1 Run a 5½" × 8½" (14cm × 21.6cm) piece of white shimmer through the Sizzix Big Shot to create the pop-up tag.

2 Pop out the die-cut pieces. Start with the piece that has a window in it. Fold along the score lines and then adhere the tabs closed to create a band at one end.

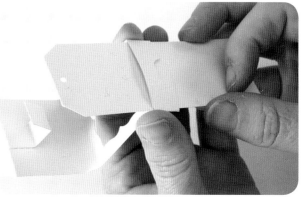

3 Adhere the three-sided loose tab piece to the perforated area.

4 Slide the flat tag into the band of the window piece.

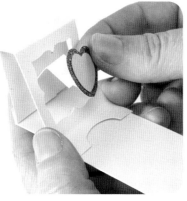

5 Adhere the notched tag pieces together with the tab of the flat tag facing down.

6 Adhere a heart embellishment (see **The Basics,** step 7) to the three-sided tab.

7 Lay the pop-up flat and adhere a gold 50 in the window. Use foam adhesive to adhere the pop-up embellishment to the card.

All Occasions

SOMETIMES YOU JUST need a simple little card to let a friend know you are thinking of her or to thank a neighbor for helping you out. This chapter is full of such cards that will not only express your gratitude but also light up the day of the recipient.

Our butterfly spiral card, for example, unexpectedly springs to life when opened. We also have pinwheels that spin in the breeze and handmade shaker cards filled with butterflies, flowers and beads.

Is your friend a bird aficionado? Try one of several cards that are sure to charm her. There are so many different ways to bring a friend cheer, and this is the chapter you don't want to miss because it is chock-full of ideas you can use over and over again to let your loved ones know that no matter how far away you might be, they are always in your thoughts.

Pinwheel Spinner Card

By Kimber McGray

Nothing screams childhood fun more than a pinwheel spinning in a light breeze. Share that childhood memory with a friend by sending this fresh and fun card.

WHAT YOU'LL NEED

- ✪ Cardstock
- ✪ Paper trimmer
- ✪ Patterned paper
- ✪ Corner rounder
- ✪ Craft knife
- ✪ Adhesive
- ✪ Foam adhesive
- ✪ Ribbon
- ✪ Adgesive dots
- ✪ Wood skewer
- ✪ Thumbtack or paper piercer
- ✪ Brad
- ✪ Pencil
- ✪ Pennies

Materials List *cardstock:* Jillibean Soup, *pattern paper:* Pink Paislee, Jillibean Soup; *ribbon:* Stampin' Up!; *punch:* EK Success; *brad:* Making Memories; *skewer:* Kitchen Supply

The Basics

1. Create a standard A2 card base (4¼" × 5½" [10.8cm × 14cm]) from kraft cardstock.

2. Cut a piece of blue patterned paper to 4" × 4" (10.2cm × 10.2cm) and round the top corners of the piece.

3. Cut a piece of green patterned paper to 4" × 2½" (10.2cm × 6.4cm) and fringe the top edge to look like grass.

4. Adhere the green patterned paper to the blue patterned paper, fringed edge overlapping the blue paper so that as a single piece, the paper measures 4" × 5¼" (10.2cm × 13.3cm). Adhere this piece to the card base with foam adhesive.

5. Slip a piece of white ribbon behind the green patterned paper and tie it into a bow.

6. Follow steps 1–4 in **Beyond the Basics** to create a pinwheel. Adhere the pinwheel to the card with an adhesive dot.

7. Cut a wood skewer to 3" (7.6cm) and adhere it to the card and under the pinwheel with adhesive dots.

Beyond the Basics

To Start:
Create a standard A2 Kraft card base (4¼" × 5½" [10.8cm × 14cm]) and set it aside.

1 To create the pinwheel, cut a 3" × 3" (7.6cm × 7.6cm) piece of patterned paper. Cut in from the corners toward the center, leaving about ½" (1.3cm) uncut.

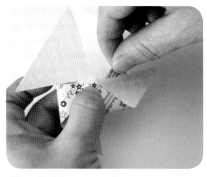

2 Fold every other corner to the center.

3 Using a thumbtack or paper piercer, pierce a hole through the center of all (five) layers.

4 Secure the layers with a brad.

5 Cut a piece of patterned paper to 4" × 3" (10.2cm x 7.6cm). Place a penny in the center of the paper and trace around it.

6 Using a craft knife, cut just inside the traced circle.

7 Adhere the patterned paper to the card base with two layers of foam adhesive.

8 Lay one penny under the hole and adhere a second penny to it with foam adhesive.

9 Adhere the pinwheel to the penny spinner with an adhesive dot.

To Finish:
Embellish the card as directed in **The Basics.**

Butterfly Shaker Card

By Lily Jackson

Butterflies are a sign of friendship and kindness. Lily's hand-cut butterfly is simply beautiful and the shaker version adds so much whimsy and fun.

WHAT YOU'LL NEED

- ✪ Cardstock
- ✪ paper trimmer
- ✪ Stamp ink pad
- ✪ Patterned paper
- ✪ Adhesive
- ✪ Circle cutter
- ✪ Twine
- ✪ Self-adhesive pearl
- ✪ Foam adhesive
- ✪ Acetate
- ✪ Scissors
- ✪ Microbeads or glitter

Materials List *cardstock:* Recollections; *patterned paper:* BoBunny Press; *stamp:* Hero Arts; *pearls:* Recollections; *microbeads:* Martha Stewart; *acetate:* Avery; *twine:* Jillibean Soup

The Basics

1. Create a 4¼" × 4¼" (10.8cm × 10.8cm) card base from Kraft cardstock.

2. Stamp a butterfly in the center of the card with brown ink.

3. Mat together two pieces of patterned paper cut to 3" × 3" (7.6cm × 7.6cm) and 3¼" × 3¼" (8.3cm × 8.3cm). Cut a 2" (5cm) hole in the center of the matted piece, and embellish the piece with twine and a self-adhesive pearl.

4. Using foam adhesive, adhere the piece over the stamped butterfly.

5. Stamp another butterfly with brown ink on a scrap of Kraft cardstock and cut it out. Adhere the butterfly cutout to the center of the card with two layers of foam adhesive. Slightly bend up the wings for added dimension.

116

Beyond the Basics

To Start:

Create a 4¼" × 4¼" (10.8cm × 10.8cm) card base from Kraft cardstock and stamp a butterfly with brown ink in the center of the card. Then...

1 Mat together two pieces of patterned paper cut to 3" × 3" (7.6cm × 7.6cm) and 3¼" × 3¼" (8.3cm × 8.3cm). Cut a 2" (5cm) hole in the center of the matted paper to create a shaker top.

2 Cut a piece of acetate to 3" × 3" (7.6cm × 7.6cm) and adhere it to the back of the matted paper shaker top. Embellish this piece with twine and a self-adhesive pearl.

3 Place foam adhesive around the edges of the shaker top. Fill the top with microbeads or glitter.

4 Adhere the card base to the shaker top.

Butterfly Spiral Card

By Kimber McGray

This vintage-inspired card brings instant warmth to any message and it really couldn't be easier to make!

WHAT YOU'LL NEED

- Cardstock
- Paper trimmer
- Patterned paper
- Adhesive
- Scalloped sticker strip
- Buttons
- Stickers
- Die cuts
- Scissors
- Adhesive dots
- Craft knife

Materials List *cardstock:* Core'dinations; *patterned paper:* Crate Paper; *stickers:* Crate Paper; *buttons:* Jenni Bowlin Studio, Stampin' Up!; *butterflies:* Jenni Bowlin Studio

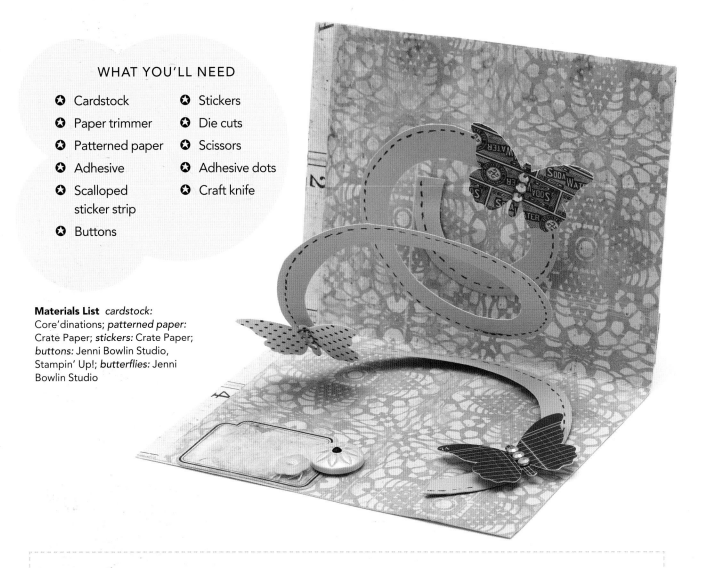

The Basics

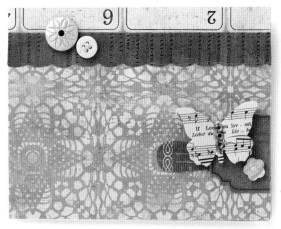

1. Create a standard A2 card base (4¼" × 5½" [10.8cm × 14cm]) from white cardstock.
2. Cut a piece of yellow patterned paper to 3¼" × 5½" (8.3cm × 14cm) and adhere it to the bottom edge of the card.
3. Cut a strip of cream patterned paper to 1" × 5½" (2.5cm × 14cm) and adhere it to the top edge of the card.
4. Place a scalloped sticker over the area where the patterned papers meet.
5. Embellish the card with buttons, stickers and a die-cut butterfly.

Beyond the Basics

To Start:

Create the basic card following all steps for **The Basics.** Cut a piece of yellow patterned paper (the same paper used on the front of the card) to 8½" × 5½" (21.6cm × 14cm) and adhere it to the interior of the card. Embellish the interior of the card with a sticker and buttons. Then...

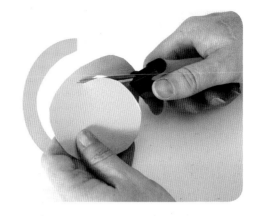

1 Cut a 4" (10.3cm) circle from yellow cardstock. Cut the circle into a ½" (1.3cm) wide spiral.

2 Cut a 1½" (3.8cm) circle out of the center of the spiral.

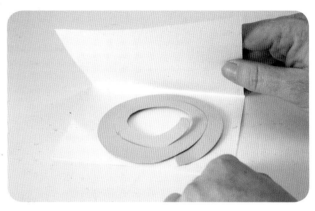

3 Adhere the outside end of the spiral to the bottom of the interior of the card (use an adhesive dot).

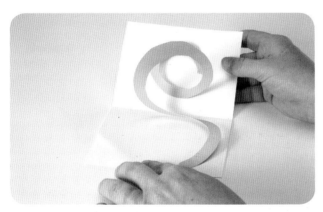

4 Adhere the inside end of the spiral to the top of the interior of the card. Place an adhesive dot on the end in the middle and simply close the card. This will adhere the spiral in the correct spot in the card.

5 Embellish the open spiral with butterfly die cuts.

Sweet Tweet Birdie Card

By Sarah Hodgkinson

A sunny greeting with a sweet birdie will make any friend smile. To make the card just a bit more "tweet," set your bird free, allowing him to flit about, spreading cheer.

WHAT YOU'LL NEED

- Cardstock
- paper trimmer
- Patterned paper
- Adhesive
- Needle and thread
- Pencil
- Craft knife
- Gem or brad
- Sandpaper
- Sewing machine
- Foam adhesive
- Button
- Twine
- Scalloped circle punch
- Circle cutter
- Quilling die (optional)

Materials List *cardstock:* Core'dinations, Jillibean Soup; *patterned paper:* Jillibean Soup; *twine:* Jillibean Soup; *button:* Creative Imaginations; *punch:* Stampin' Up!; *adhesive:* foam adhesive; *other tools:* Imaginisce Hot Rocks, Provo Craft/Cuttlebug paper quilling die, Hot Off the Press bird template, Creative Memories circle cutting system, Core'dinations Sand It Gadget

The Basics

1. Create a 6" × 6" (15.2cm × 15.2cm) square card base from kraft cardstock.
2. Cut a piece of cloud patterned paper to 5½" × 5½" (14cm × 14cm), and adhere it to the card base.
3. From each of four different shades of green cardstock, cut a strip to ¾" × 5¾" (2cm × 14cm). Hand cut fringe or use a paper quilling die to create "grass." Adhere the pieces to the cards, layering one atop the next.
4. Sew a border with white thread ⅜" (1cm) in from the edge of the Kraft card base.
5. Using the templates on page 137, trace and cut out the bird and wing from patterned paper. Assemble the bird. Attach a black gem or brad for the bird's eye.
6. Cut a half circle of orange cardstock for the bird's chest. Trim the paper to fit, and lightly sand the edges.
7. Attach the bird to the card with foam adhesive.
8. Punch a scalloped circle from yellow cardstock. Thread a large yellow button with twine and adhere it to the scalloped circle. Adhere the circle to the card.

Beyond the Basics

To Start:
Create a 6" × 6" (15.2cm × 15.2cm) card base out of Kraft cardstock. Then...

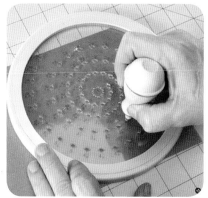

1 Cut a piece of patterned paper to 5½" × 5½" (14cm × 14cm), and cut a 3½" (9cm) circle from the center.

2 Cut a 3¼" (8.3cm) circle from the front of the Kraft card base.

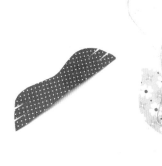

3 Using the templates on page 137, trace two birds and wings, and cut the pieces out.

4 Adhere the two bird pieces together with a 7" (17.8cm) piece of twine sandwiched between them.

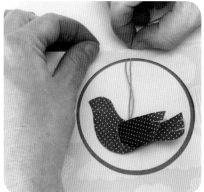

5 Slide the wings through the slots in the bird's body.

6 Adhere the twine between the card base and the patterned paper, centering the bird in the hole.

To Finish:
Embellish the card by following steps 3, 6 and 7 from **The Basics,** and add a black gem or brad for the bird's eye.

Thinking of You Slider Card

By Rae Barthel

Without rain, there are no rainbows. This sweet card is perfect for sending a note of encouragement to a friend.

WHAT YOU'LL NEED

- Cardstock
- Paper trimmer
- Patterned paper
- Adhesive
- Ribbon
- Button
- Pencil
- Craft knife
- Bone folder
- Circle punch

Materials List *cardstock:* Bazzill Basics; *patterned paper:* Nikki Sivils Scrapbooker; *buttons:* Nikki Sivils Scrapbooker; *ribbon:* Papertrey Ink; *pen:* Sharpie; *punch:* EK Success

The Basics

1. Create a 4½" × 6" (11.4cm × 15.2cm) card base from white cardstock.

2. Cut a piece of blue patterned paper to 4" × 5½" (10.2cm × 14cm) and adhere it to the card base.

3. Wrap a gingham ribbon around the cover of the card and tie it into a bow. Embellish the center of the bow with a button.

4. Cut out clouds and a turtle from patterned paper and adhere the pieces to the card.

Beyond the Basics

To Start:
Create a 6" × 4½" (15.2cm × 11.4cm) card base out of white cardstock and set it aside. (This piece will be your slider base.)Then...

1 On the back of the piece, draw a rectangle 1" (3cm) from the left, ¾" (2.5cm) from the top and bottom and ½" (1.3cm) from the right. Draw a line through the center of the rectangle. Cut along the top, right and bottom edges.

2 Score along the center and left lines.

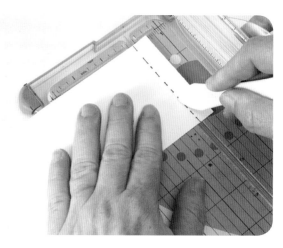

3 Cut a piece of white cardstock to 6" × 3" (15.2cm × 7.6cm). This will be the slider. Score ½" (1.3cm) from the right edge and fold.

4 Adhere the ½" (1.3cm) tab of the slider into the open end of the slider base.

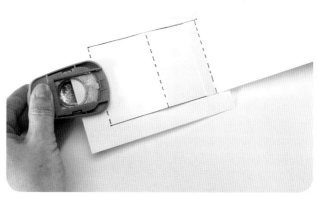

5 Using a circle punch, notch out a half circle on the left edge of the slider base.

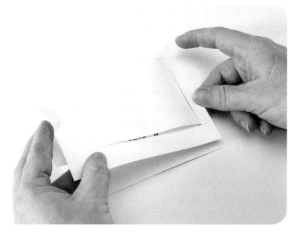

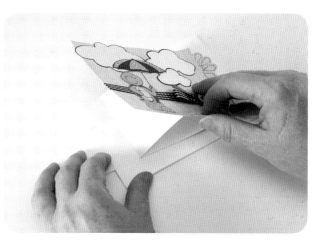

6 Fold the slider tab on the far right toward the back of the card. Adhere the slider base to the card base, adhering only the top, bottom and right sides, and allowing the slider tab to slide through the opening on the left side.

7 Create a patterned paper panel following steps 2, 3 and 4 from **The Basics**, and adhere this patterned paper panel to the top panel on the right.

8 Pull on the slider tab to expose the empty panel underneath. Embellish with a rainbow and sun hand cut from patterned paper.

The Flower and the Bee Card

By Kim Hughes

A bright and cheery tulip will brighten anyone's day, but watch out—a bee may spring from inside the flower. Don't fret, he just wants to wish you a great day!

WHAT YOU'LL NEED

- ✪ Cardstock
- ✪ Paper trimmer
- ✪ Border punch
- ✪ Patterned paper
- ✪ Adhesive
- ✪ Twine
- ✪ Tape
- ✪ Pencil
- ✪ Scissors or craft knife
- ✪ Stamp
- ✪ Ink pad
- ✪ Wire
- ✪ Adhesive dot

Materials List *cardstock:* Bazzill Basics; *patterned paper:* Imaginisce, My Mind's Eye, American Crafts, Echo Park Paper; *stamp:* Paper Smooches; *ink:* Memento by Tsukineko; *wire:* Craft Supply; *twine:* Creative Impressions

The Basics

1. Create a standard A2 card base (4¼" × 5½" [10.8cm × 14cm]) from yellow cardstock.
2. Cut a 4" × 5" (10.2cm × 12.7cm) piece of tan cardstock, scallop one edge and adhere it to the card.
3. Adhere a 1½" × 5½" (3.8cm × 14cm) piece of blue patterned paper to the left edge of the card (covering part of the piece of tan cardstock).
4. Adhere a 3" (7.6cm) piece of twine to the card, securing with tape. (Wrap the bottom of the twine into the card.)
5. Cut a tulip (use the template on page 138) and a leaf from patterned paper. Adhere the pieces to the card as shown in the photo on the left. Bend the edges of the leaf away from the card for dimension.

Beyond the Basics

To Start:

Make the card as directed in **The Basics,** but do not adhere the tulip shape to the card quite yet. Instead...

1 Stamp and cut out a bee image. (I used black ink.)

2 Create a pocket by adhering the tulip to the card along the edges only.

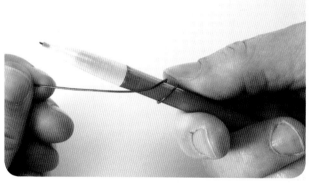

3 Coil a piece of wire (about 6" [15.2cm]) around a pencil and then press to flatten the coiled wire.

4 Adhere the bee to end of wire and then use n adhesive dot to adhere the wire inside the tulip pocket.

Flower Shaker Card

By Kimber McGray

A fun color combination makes the flower stand out on this quick and simple card.

WHAT YOU'LL NEED

- Cardstock
- Paper trimmer
- Corner rounder
- Border punch
- Patterned paper
- Adhesive
- Twine
- Foam adhesive
- Circle and flower punches
- Self-adhesive pearls
- Acetate
- Scissors
- Small beads or glitter

Materials List *cardstock:* Jillibean Soup, Core'dinations; *patterned paper:* Jillibean Soup; *twine:* Jillibean Soup; *punches:* Stampin' Up!, Marvy Uchida, EK Success; *acetate:* Avery; *pearls:* Queen & Co.; *seed beads:* Craft Supply; *foam adhesive squares:* 3L Scrapbook Adhesives

The Basics

1. Create a standard A2 card base (4¼" × 5½" [10.8cm × 14cm]) from Kraft cardstock.
2. Cut a piece of white cardstock to 5" × 3¾" (12.7cm × 9.5cm). Round the corners with a corner rounder.
3. Cut a strip of green cardstock to ½" × 5" (1.3cm × 12.7cm) and scallop one edge. Cut a piece of blue patterned paper to 1" × 5" (2.5cm × 12.7cm). Layer the green scalloped strip behind the

blue paper and adhere the two together. Adhere this piece to the white cardstock.
4. Wrap a piece of twine around the white cardstock twice and tie it into a bow. Adhere the white cardstock panel to the front of the card base with foam adhesive.
5. Punch a flower (or a scalloped circle) from orange patterned paper and a 1½" (3.8cm) circle from blue patterned paper. Layer the circle

onto the flower and adhere the two together. Adhere the flower to the card with foam adhesive. Add a few red self-adhesive pearls to the center of the flower.

Beyond the Basics

To Start:
Follow steps 1–4 of **The Basics.** Then...

1 Punch out a patterned paper circle with a 1½" (3.8cm) circle punch.

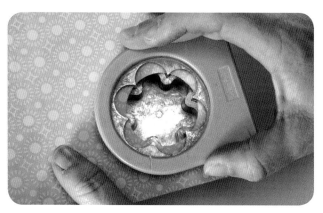

2 Use another paper punch (this one is a 2" [5cm] scalloped circle) to punch out a flower shape directly over the hole left in the patterned paper from step 1.

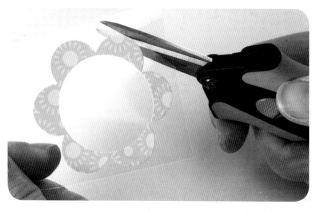

3 Adhere the punched flower to a piece of acetate and trim around the edges of the flower with scissors.

4 Place foam adhesive around the edges of the acetate window. Fill this piece with small beads or glitter.

5 Punch a 1¾" (4.5cm) circle from coordinating cardstock and adhere it to the back of the acetate window.

To Finish:
Use foam adhesive to adhere the shaker to the card.

Birdhouse Card

By Kim Hughes

This is a great little card to send to a friend to let her know you are thinking of her.

WHAT YOU'LL NEED

- Cardstock
- Paper trimmer
- Patterned paper
- Border punch
- Adhesive
- Corrugated die-cut frame and bird
- Paint
- Flower or asterisk punch
- Self-adhesive gems
- Glue
- Pencil
- Craft knife
- Straight pin

Materials List *cardstock:* Bazzill Basics; *patterned paper:* Echo Park Paper, Crate Paper; *corrugated shapes:* Jillibean Soup; *paint:* Making Memories; *punches:* EK Success, Stampin' Up!; *gems:* Queen & Co.

The Basics

1. Create a 5" × 5" (12.7cm × 12.7cm) card base from white cardstock.
2. Cut a strip of pink patterned paper to 1" × 5" (2.5cm × 12.7cm) and scallop the edge. Adhere the strip to the right edge of the card, overhanging the card by about ¼" (6mm).
3. Cut a piece of floral patterned paper to 5" × 5" (12.7cm ×12.7cm) and adhere it over the card base, aligning it with the left edge of the card base. The ¼" (6mm) scalloped strip along the right edge of the card should be exposed.
4. Cut a piece of pink patterned paper to 2" × 2" (5cm × 5cm) and adhere it to the back of a die-cut corrugated frame. Adhere the window to the card front.
5. Paint a corrugated bird and, when dry, adhere it to the card.
6. Punch three flowers from yellow patterned paper (using an asterisk punch works well), embellish the flowers with adhesive-backed gems and adhere the flowers to the card with glue.

Beyond the Basics

To Start:
Follow steps 1–3 of **The Basics.** Then...

1 Lay the die-cut window on the card.

2 Trace around the inside hole of the die-cut with a pencil. Cut out the hole with a craft knife, and adhere the die-cut window around the hole, creating a framed window.

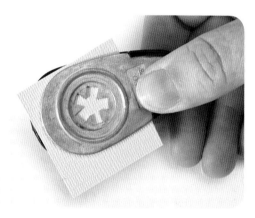

3 Punch three small flowers from yellow cardstock. (I love to use an asterisk punch for this.)

4 Adhere one of the punched flowers to the top of a straight pin with a glue dot.

5 Embellish the fronts of the punched flowers with self-adhesive gems.

6 Insert into and/or adhere the flowers to the die-cut frame. Finish embellishing the card by adhering a die-cut bird.

Tri-Fold Flower Card

By Kimber McGray

Polka dots and butterflies never fail to brighten up even the gloomiest of days.

Materials List *cardstock:* Core'dinations; *patterned paper:* Studio Calico, Pebbles Inc.; *punches:* Stampin' Up!, EK Success; *brad:* Pebbles Inc.

The Basics

1. Create a standard A2 card base (4¼" × 5½" [10.8cm × 14cm]) from cream cardstock.
2. Cut a piece of orange patterned paper to 3¾" × 5" (9.5cm × 12.7cm) and adhere it to the card.
3. Cut a piece of cream cardstock to 2½" × 3½" (6.4cm × 9cm). Scallop one end of the cardstock and adhere it to the card.
4. Cut out a few butterflies from patterned paper and adhere them to the card with foam adhesive.
5. Create the accordion flower embellishment by following steps 4–9 in **Beyond the Basics.**
6. Adhere the accordion flower to the front of the card.

WHAT YOU'LL NEED

- Cardstock
- Paper trimmer
- Patterned paper
- Adhesive
- Border punch
- Foam adhesive
- Craft knife
- Bone folder
- Scoring board
- Circle punch
- Button or other embellishment

Beyond the Basics

1 Create a card base by cutting a piece of cardstock to 5½" × 8" (14cm × 20.3cm). Score 2" (5cm) from the edge on both of the 5½" (14cm) sides.

2 Fold the flaps in.

3 Cut two pieces of patterned paper to 1¾" × 5" (4.5cm × 12.7cm). Adhere them to the card, lining them up with the opening. Cut a piece of cardstock to 3" × 2" (7.6cm × 5cm), scallop one of the short edges, and adhere it to the left side of the card so that it overlaps the right side of the card.

4 To create the accordion flower embellishment, cut a strip of patterned paper to 1" × 12" 2.5cm × 30.5cm). Score the paper at ½" (1.3cm) intervals.

5 Accordion fold the paper along the score lines.

6 Adhere the ends of the accordion together.

7 Press the accordion flower flat onto a table or other work surface with the back side facing up.

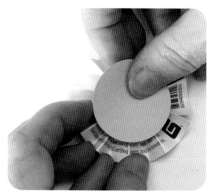

8 Punch a 1½" (3.8cm) circle from cardstock and adhere it to the back of the accordion flower.

9 Add a small embellishment to the front of the flower.

10 Adhere the accordion flower embellishment to the cardstock flap on the front of the card.

Hinged Ladybug Card

By Kimber McGray

It's said that you will have good luck if a ladybug lands on you. Send your own bit of good luck with a sweet ladybug featured front and center.

WHAT YOU'LL NEED

- ✪ Cardstock
- ✪ Paper trimmer
- ✪ Patterned paper
- ✪ Circle cutter or punches
- ✪ Black pen
- ✪ Adhesive
- ✪ Paper piercer or thumbtack
- ✪ Brad
- ✪ Bone folder

Materials List *cardstock:* Core'dinations; *patterned paper:* Jillibean Soup; *brad:* Making Memories; *punches:* Marvy Uchida, EK Success; *pen:* Zig; *foam adhesive squares:* 3L Scrapbook Adhesives

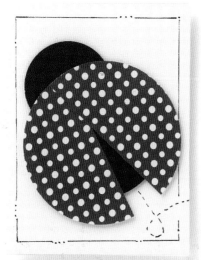

The Basics

1. Create a standard A2 card base (4¼" × 5½" [10.8cm × 14cm]) from white cardstock.
2. Hand draw a border around the perimeter of the card with a black pen.
3. Punch out and adhere a 3" (7.6cm) black cardstock circle over a 2" (5cm) black cardstock circle. Adhere the circles to the front of the card for the ladybug body.
4. Punch a 3½" (9cm) circle from polka dot patterned paper. Cut the circle in half and adhere the halves over the black ladybug body, opening and overlapping the wings slightly.
5. Draw a few dashed lines on the cardstock to show the path of the ladybug.

Beyond the Basics

1 Punch two circles from black cardstock, one 3" (7.6cm) and one 2" (5cm). Adhere the 3" (7.6cm) circle to the 2" (5cm) circle.

2 Punch a 3½" (9cm) circle from red patterned paper and cut the circle in half for the wings.

3 Lay the wings on the larger black circle so the ends overlap slightly, and pierce all the layers with a thumbtack.

4 Attach the wings to the body with a red brad.

5 Punch another 3" (7.6cm) circle from black cardstock. Score ½" (1.3cm) from the edge, as shown.

6 Fold on the ½" (1.3cm) score line to create a tab. Adhere the tab to the back of ladybug (line it up with the other 3" [7.6cm] black circle) to create the card base.

Templates

(line this edge on paper fold line)

New Home Gift Card Holder

(page 94)

(enlarge all by 125%)

(line this edge on paper fold line)

(line this edge on paper fold line)

Congrats Honeycomb Stars Card

(page 96)

(enlarge all by 118%)

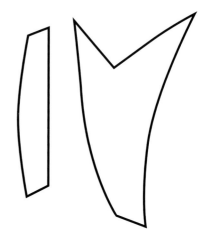

Stocking Gift Card Holder

(page 46)

(enlarge all by 125%)

Make a Wish Card
(page 28)
(enlarge all by 125%)

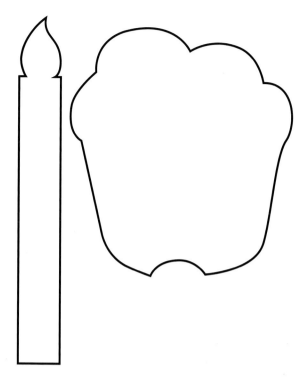

Sweet Tweet Birdie Card
(page 120)
(enlarge all by 118%)

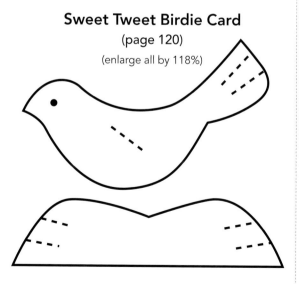

From the "Little Birdies" template by
Susan Niner Janes for *Hot Off the Press*

Cupcake Gift Card Holder
(page 38)
(enlarge all by 118%)

Templates (continued)

The Flower and the Bee Card
(page 68)
(at 100%)

Template courtesy Kim Hughes,
Paper Smooches Stamps

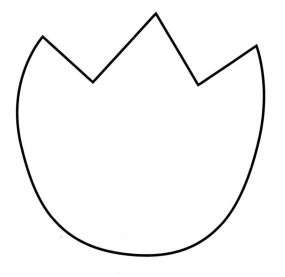

Birthday Gifts and Balloon Card
(page 22)
(at 100%)

Easter Chick Card
(page 68)
(at 100%)

Templates courtesy Kim Hughes,
Paper Smooches Stamps

New Wheels Scooter Pull Card
(page 106)
(at 100%)

Template courtesy Kim Hughes,
Paper Smooches Stamps

About the Contributors

Rae Barthel

Rae, 40 years young, is from Chicago and now lives in Huntsville, Alabama. She is wife to Tom and mother to Michael, Lauren and Matthew. She is a daughter, a sister and a cardmaker. Rae has been designing cards for eight years and is enjoying every moment of her papercrafting journey, from winning the *Paper Crafts* Gallery Idol title in 2009, to seeing her work appear among the pages of her favorite card making publications. Rae loves this hobby and is thrilled to share her work with you! Check out her blog: simplyrae.blogspot.com.

Summer Fullerton

Summer is a *Creative Keepsakes* Hall of Fame winner and a Memory Makers Master. She has been paper crafting for more than thirteen years. Summer lives with her husband and two children just south of Portland, Oregon. She is the co-author of *Remember This* and currently designs for *Scrapbook & Cards Today* and Jillibean Soup. When she is not shuttling her kids around or papercrafting, she also enjoys cooking, sewing, photography and the occasional round of golf. Find out what Summer is up to now: summerfullerton.typepad.com.

Sarah Hodgkinson

Sarah lives in Woodstock, Ontario with her husband, two children and dog. She is a teacher who enjoys spending her free time with scissors, glue and paper. Sarah currently serves on several design teams including Core'dinations, *Scrapbook & Cards Today* magazine, All About Scrapbooks & More and Custom Crops. She has been published in many crafting magazines and enjoys teaching at events including ScrapFest and CreativFestival. Visit Sarah's blog: thehodgeesonlyinhollywoodstock. blogspot.com.

Kim Hughes

Kim was born in New York and currently lives in Arizona with her wonderful family of seven. She has loved art her whole life but found paper crafting about twelve years ago. She's been hooked ever since.Kim has worked with numerous manufactures, stores and magazines, and she is now owns her own store, Paper Smooches. All Paper Smooches stamps are designed by Kim. When she has the time, Kim LOVES to make cards! Want to know more? Go to: paper-smooches.blogspot.com.

Lisa Dorsey

Lisa was born and raised in Wisconsin and currently lives in Indiana. She and her fabulous husband have two daughters. Lisa started scrapbooking more ten years ago following a family vacation. In no time she became truly, madly passionate about it, spending more and more time scrapbooking and submitting her work for publication. Since then, she has been fortunate to have her layouts, cards and projects published in many of the major magazines. Lisa is currently a designer for Emma's Paperie online store, Creative Charms and Sizzix. You can catch up with her at: lisadorsey.blogspot.com.

Kelly Goree

Kelly lives in the beautiful horse country of Kentucky with her husband and their three rambunctious boys. She began scrapbooking in 2000, just after her oldest son was born. She'll tell you if she's not out chasing her boys, you can find her scrapping! Kelly is a full-time staff designer and international instructor for BasicGrey. She is a *Memory Makers* Master and has been published more than 500 times. Visit Kelly's blog to see what she's working on: kellygoree.blogspot.com.

Lily Jackson

Lily has enjoyed working on creative projects from a young age. Whether it is making pottery, drawing, or sewing, she has always had a creative outlet. She received a Young Artist Award at age eleven, and two years later, her work was published in *Simply Handmade Magazine*. In 2008, she discovered the world of scrapbooking and cardmaking. In her free time, Lily loves to make and share her work on YouTube. You can find her at: www.youtube.com/msscrappingal.

Nichol Magouirk

Nichol is a *Creating Keepsakes* Hall of Famer and a member of the *BHG Scrapbooks, Etc.* creative team. She has been published in many different scrapbooking publications and idea books and has contributed to several manufacturers' design teams. . Her favorite techniques are die cutting and stamping. Nichol lives in Kansas with her husband of fourteen years and their three children. Nichol regularly updates her blog with new projects and how-to videos, so be sure to check it out: www.nicholmagouirk.typepad.com.

Resources

The following companies manufacture products featured in this book. Please check your local retailers to find these materials, or go to a company's website for the latest product information. In addition, we have made every attempt to properly credit the items mentioned in this book. We apologize to any company that we have listed incorrectly, and we would appreciate hearing from you.

3L Corporation—Scrapbook Adhesives
www.scrapbook-adhesives.com

Alterred Bits
www.Alteredbits.com

American Crafts
www.americancrafts.com

Avery
www.avery.com

BasicGrey
www.basicgrey.com

Bazzill Basics Paper
www.bazzillbasics.com

Bella Blvd
www.bellablvd.net

BoBunny Press
www.bobunny.com

Buttons Galore
www.buttonsgaloreandmore.com

Canvas Corp
www.canvascorp.com

Clearsnap, Inc.
www.clearsnap.com

Coats & Clark
www.coatsandclark.com

Colorbox
www.colorbox.com

Copic Markers
www.copicmarker.com

Core'dinations
www.coredinations.com

Cosmo Cricket
www.cosmocricket.com

Crate Paper, Inc.
www.cratepaper.com

Creative Charms
www.creativecharms.com

Creative Imaginations
www.cigift.com

Creative Impressions
www.creativeimpressions.com

Creative Memories
www.creativememories.com

Darice
www.darcie.com

DCWV
www.diecutswithaview.com

Divine Twine
www.whiskergraphics.com

DMC Corp.
www.dmc-usa.com

Doodlebug Design, Inc.
www.doodlebug.ws

Echo Park Paper
www.echoparkpaper.com

EK Success, Ltd.
www.eksuccess.com

Fancy Pants Designs, LLC
www.fancypantsdesigns.com

Fiskars, Inc.
www.fiskars.com

Gina K Designs
www.ginakdesigns.ning.com

Glue Dots International
www.gluedots.com

Hero Arts Rubber Stamps, Inc.
www.heroarts.com

Hobby Lobby
www.hobbylobby.com

Horizon Fabric
www.horizongroupusa.com

Hot Off the Press–*see* **Paper Wishes**

Imaginisce
www.imaginisce.com

Inkadinkado
www.eksuccessbrands.com/inkadinkado

Inky Antics
www.inkyantics.com

Jenni Bowlin
www.jennibowlin.com

Jillibean Soup
www.jillibean-soup.com

Jo-Ann Fabric and Craft Stores
www.joann.com

Jolee's Boutique—*see* **EK Success, Ltd.**

K&Company
www.kandcompany.com

KI Memories, Inc,
www.kimemories.com

Kitchen Supply
www.kitchensupply.com

Lawn Fawn
www.lawnfawn.com

Making Memories
www.makingmemories.com

Martha Stewart Crafts
www.marthastewartcrafts.com

Marvy Uchida/Uchida of America, Corp.
www.uchida.com

Maya Road, LLC
www.mayaroad.com

May Arts
www.mayarts.com

Michaels Stores
www.michaels.com

Momenta
www.momenta.com

My Mind's Eye, Inc.
www.mymindseye.com

Neenah Paper, Inc.
www.neenahpaper.com

Nikki Sivilis, Scrapbooker
www.nikkisivilis.com

Our Craft Lounge
www.ourcraftlounge.net

Paper Smooches
www.papersmoochesstamps.com

The Paper Studio
www.paperstudio.com

Paper Wishes
PaperWishes.com

Papertrey Ink
www.papertreyink.com

Pebbles Inc.
www.pebblesinc.com

Pepperell
www.pepperell.com

Pink Paislee
www.pinkpaislee.com

Prima Marketing, Inc.
www.primamarketinginc.com

Provo Craft
www.provocraft.com

Queen & Co.
www.queenandcompany.com

QuicKutz, Inc.
www.quickutz.com

Ranger Industries, Inc.
www.rangerink.com

Recollections
www.recollectionsonline.com

Sakura of America
www.sakuraofamerica.com

Scor-Pal
www.scor-pal.com

SEI, Inc.
www.shopsei.com

Silhouette America
www.silhouetteamerica.com

Singer
www.singerco.com

Sizzix
www.sizzix.com

Spellbinders Paper Arts, LLC
www.spellbinders.us

Stampin' Up!
www.stampinup.com

Studio Calico
www.studiocalico.com

Tim Holtz
www.timholtz.com

Tsukineko, LLC
www.tsukineko.com

Uni-ball/Sanford
www.uniball-na.com

Unity Stamp Company
www.unitystampco.com

We R Memory Keepers
www.weronthenet.com

Xyron
www.xyon.com

Zig
www.kuretake.co.uk

Zva Creative
www.zvacreative.com

Index

About the Author

Kimber McGray is a 2007 *Creating Keepsakes* Hall of Fame Winner who teaches at local scrapbook stores and guest teaches at other locations across the United States and Canada. She currently works on the design teams for the following manufacturers and regularly attends CHA with them: Jillibean Soup, Core'dinations and Unity Stamp Company. Kimber is coauthor of *Remember This*, the author of *Scrapbook Secrets* and *175 Fresh Card Ideas* and has contributed artwork and articles to numerous other books and magazines. Visit her blog: kimbermcgray.blogspot.com

Dedication

This book is dedicated to my incredible husband, Bill, who has been incredibly supportive during this crazy process of writing my fourth book in four years. Thank you for allowing me to try new adventures and enjoy this hobby.

Acknowledgments

The best part of the paper-crafting hobby is learning new things and exploring ideas to see how they turn out. In writing this book and working on different projects over the past year, I have been given an 'excuse' to try new techniques and create projects I have never done before. Creating with paper is very forgiving because if you don't succeed on your first try, simply grab another piece of paper and try again. While working on this book, I discovered so many great ways to push, pull and spin paper that I had never thought of before. Now my head is exploding with so many more ideas just waiting to come to life.

I first want to thank my family for continuing to encourage me and being so very understanding when I had hectic deadlines to meet. I love you.

To my contributors, your creativity helped drive me and kept me motivated while working on this book. Your enthusiasm to create fun and exciting cards on short deadlines made working with you an extreme pleasure. Also, thank you allowing me to donate all of these wonderful cards to the Ronald McDonald House of Indiana. The families and children will enjoy each and every one of your beautiful creations.

Also, thanks goes to Christine Doyle for allowing me to create another book with F+W Media, your patience in listening to my millions of different ideas is impressive. To my editor Kristy Conlin, thank you for trusting in me. And finally to my wonderful photographer Christine Polomsky, doing the photo shoots are always so much fun and easy to do.

Fresh and Fun Handmade Cards. Copyright © 2012 by Kimber McGray. Manufactured in China. All rights reserved. No part of this book may be reproduced in any form or by any electronic or mechanical means including information storage and retrieval systems without permission in writing from the publisher, except by a reviewer who may quote brief passages in a review. Published by North Light Books, an imprint of F+W Media, Inc., 10151 Carver Road, Cincinnati, Ohio, 45236. (800) 289-0963. First Edition.

media

www.fwmedia.com

16 15 14 13 12 5 4 3 2 1

DISTRIBUTED IN CANADA BY FRASER DIRECT
100 Armstrong Avenue
Georgetown, ON, Canada L7G 5S4
Tel: (905) 877-4411

DISTRIBUTED IN THE U.K. AND EUROPE BY F+W MEDIA INTERNATIONAL
Brunel House, Newton Abbot, Devon, TQ12 4PU, England
Tel: (+44) 1626 323200, Fax: (+44) 1626 323319
Email: postmaster@davidandcharles.co.uk

DISTRIBUTED IN AUSTRALIA BY CAPRICORN LINK
P.O. Box 704, S. Windsor NSW, 2756 Australia
Tel: (02) 4577-3555

ISBN: 978-1-4403-1499-5
SRN: W2288

Edited by	Kristy Conlin
Designed by	Ronson Slagle
Production coordinated by	Greg Nock
Photography by	Christine Polomsky and Al Parrish
Styling by	Lauren Emmerling

Metric Conversion Chart

To convert	to	multiply by
Inches	Centimeters	2.54
Centimeters	Inches	0.4
Feet	Centimeters	30.5
Centimeters	Feet	0.03
Yards	Meters	0.9
Meters	Yards	1.1